Jaina Contribution to Varanasi

Jaina Contribution to Varanasi

Editors

R.C. Sharma
Pranati Ghosal

Jñāna-Pravāha
Centre for Cultural Studies and Research
Varanasi

D.K. Printworld (P) Ltd.
New Delhi

Cataloging in Publication Data — DK
[Courtesy: D.K. Agencies (P) Ltd. <docinfo@dkagencies.com>]

Jaina contribution to Varanasi / edited by
R.C. Sharma, Pranati Ghosal.
x, 166 p. 23 cm.
Contributed articles.
Includes passages in Sanskrit (roman)
Includes bibliographical references.
Includes index.
ISBN 8124603413

1. Jainism — India — Varanasi — History. 2. Jaina art — India — Varanasi. I. Sharma, R.C., 1936- II. Ghosal, Pranati, 1956-.

DDC 294.409 542 21

ISBN 81-246-0341-3
First Published in India in 2006

Published by:
Jñāna Pravāha
Centre for Cultural Studies and Research
South of Samne Ghat, Varanasi - 221 005
Phones : (0542) 236 6326; *Fax* : (0542) 236 6971
E-mail: jpvns@satyam.net.in
Web: www.jnanapravha.org

and

D.K. Printworld (P) Ltd.
Regd. office : *"Sri Kunj,"* F-52, Bali Nagar,
New Delhi - 110 015
Phones : (011) 2545-3975; 2546-6019; *Fax* : (011) 2546-5926
E-mail: dkprintworld@vsnl.net
Web: www.dkprintworld.com

printed by: D.K. Printworld (P) Ltd., New Delhi.

Preface

VARANASI or Kāśī radiated the rays of knowledge in all the directions, and the sages, seers and preceptors have been thronging the city from time immemorial. They either aimed at seeking knowledge or disseminating their faith or testing their wisdom among the galaxy of learned scholars before the propagation of their philosophy. There was generally no barrier of any religion, creed or sect as the education was available easily for all. But sometimes the conventions compelled the seeker of knowledge to remain *in cognito*. These factors were responsible for shaping the city as a centre of different religions from a hoary past and it does continue till date.

The *Jñāna-Pravāha* has resolved to organize an annual feature under the caption of *Radiance of Kāśī*, in which contribution made by the eminent people or well-known sects can be discussed and appreciated. All have contributed in their own way in spreading the glory of the city and they have to be given due homage by the present generation. The *Jaina Contribution to Kāśī* was also a remarkable feature and the perusal of papers presented will certainly shed valuable light on various aspects of the subject.

The present book incorporates the revised and edited version of the proceedings of a two day colloquium held on April 11-12, 2000 at *Jñāna Pravāha* and coordinated by Sri Kranti Kumar. Most of the papers were presented in Hindi which have now been rendered in English.

Smt. Bimla Poddar, Founder and Managing Trustee *Jñāna Pravāha* and Sri Susheel K. Mittal of D.K. Printworld deserve deep appreciation for their keen initiative in the publication this volume. The assistance rendered by Dr. Niraj Pandey and Sri Chandraneel Sharma is also appreciated.

We conclude with a verse:

> *ahiṁsā mūlako dharmo yena saṁsthāpito bhuvi* ।
> *aparigrāhī tapo mūrtiḥ mahāvīraḥ prasīdatu* ॥

R.C. Sharma
Pranati Ghosal

Contents

List of Illustrations

Key to Transliteration

VOWELS

अ *a*	आ *ā*	इ *i*	ई *ī*	उ *u*	ऊ *ū*
(but)	(palm)	(it)	(beet)	(put)	(pool)
ऋ *ṛ*	ए *e*	ऐ *ai*	ओ *o*	औ *au*	
(rhythm)	(play)	(air)	(toe)	(loud)	

CONSONANTS

Guttural	क *ka*	ख* *kha*	ग *ga*	घ *gha*	ङ *ṅa*
	(skate)	(blockhead)	(gate)	(ghost)	(sing)
Palatal	च *ca*	छ* *cha*	ज *ja*	झ *jha*	ञ *ña*
	(chunk)	(catch him)	(john)	(hedgehog)	(bunch)
Cerebral	ट *ṭa*	ठ* *ṭha*	ड *ḍa*	ढ* *ḍha*	ण* *ṇa*
	(start)	(anthill)	(dart)	(godhead)	(under)
Dental	त *ta*	थ *tha*	द *da*	ध* *dha*	न *na*
	(path)	(thunder)	(that)	(breathe)	(numb)
Labial	प *pa*	फ* *pha*	ब *ba*	भ *bha*	म *ma*
	(spin)	(philosophy)	(bin)	(abhor)	(much)
Semi-	य *ya*	र *ra*	ल *la*	व *va*	
vowel	(young)	(drama)	(luck)	(vile)	
Sibilants	श *śa*	ष *ṣa*	स *sa*	ह *ha*	
	(shove)	(bushel)	(so)	(hum)	
Others	क्ष *kṣa*	त्र *tra*	ज्ञ *jña*	ळ* *ḷ*	ॠ* *ṝ*
		(*kṣatriya*)	(*triśūla*)	(*jñānī*)	(*play*)

अं (—̇)*ṁ anusvāra* (nasalisation of preceding vowel) like *saṁskṛti*

अः *visarga* = *ḥ* (aspiration of preceding vowel) like (*prātaḥ*)

ऽ *Avagraha* consonant #'consonant (like:- *ime 'vasthitā*)

Anusvāra at the end of a line is presented by m (म्) and not ṁ

HINDI LETTERS (extras)

ँ = *ñ*	—̇ = ṅ	ड़ = *ṛa*	ढ़ = *ṛha*
(*candrabindu*)	(*anusvāra*)		

* No exact English equivalents for these letters.

1

Jaina Contribution to Kāśī
An Introduction

Kranti Kumar

EXAMINING history at a micro level has many hazards. Particularly, when it is a rich and ancient religion like Jainism, which can definitely be said to be among the oldest living religions of the world, if not the oldest. Historically, it goes back to the eighth-seventh century BC. But if Mohenjo-Dāro writings are deciphered, and they support the view of some scholars that the seals, etc., have Jaina influence, then even known history of Jainism will get thrown back by a millennium at least. Scholars like Dr. Sagar Mal Jain have tried to link some hymns of *Ṛgveda* with Jainism or Jaina philosophy.[1] If we accept this view then one can safely say that some early form of Jainism existed as long back as the second millennium BC. To quote:

> *catvāri śṛṅgā trayo asya pādā dve śīrṣe sapta hastāso asya* ।
> *tridhā baddho vṛṣabho roravīti maho-devo martyāñ ā vivēśa* ॥
> — *Ṛgveda* 4.58.3

Dr. Jain quotes Satvalekar's translation based on Sāyaṇa in its literal form — "This *vṛṣabha* or *deva* has four horns, three legs, two heads and seven hands. This *vṛṣabha* or powerful *deva* is tied at three places and makes human beings."[2] This meaning

1. Dr. Sagarmal Jain, *Śramaṇa*, April-June 1994, p. 185.
2. *Ibid.*, p. 191.

hardly seems to be logical. Translating with Jaina thought he suggests that this can be as follows:

> *Vṛṣabha* (*Ṛṣabha*) *deva* bound by the three *yogas* of *manas*, *vacana* and *kāya* announced that Mahādeva or Supreme Lord resides in the mortals. Its four-fold form of infinite knowledge, infinite philosophy, infinite happiness and infinite power/strength (*vīrya*) are the four horns. *Samyak* knowledge, philosophy and character (of steadfastness) are the three foundations or legs. This Supreme Lord's two heads are knowledge-based and philosophy-based. Its seven hands are the five sensory perceptions and desire and intelligence.

This probably is more logical.

In another context he points out that at several places in the *Ṛgveda* the adjective used for Vṛṣabha is Marutvān (2.33.6). In Jaina tradition Ṛṣabhadeva is also acknowledged as son of Maru Devī.[3]

There are many such instances in the Vedic lore. One cannot, therefore, deny a certain relevance which probably helps Jaina traditions to date back to Ṛgvedic period. Śramaṇa and Brāhmaṇa traditions, i.e., Arhat and Barhat traditions, are frequently encountered in the *Ṛgveda*.[4] Some scholars (Late Dr. K.N. Misra) felt that Arhat and Barhat were not opposing traditions but probably indicated village/city-based culture, and forest-based (recluse) culture. This briefly points to the pre-historic antiquity of Jainism.

Now we come to Varanasi in historical times. During the last hundred years scholars, both in India and outside, have come to a definite conclusion that Pārśvanātha was a historic figure and was the king of Varanasi.[5] After abdicating the

---

3. *Ibid.*, p. 194
4. *Ibid.*, p. 186.
5. Pandit Sukhlal Sanghvi, *Cāra Tīrthaṅkara*. (Quoting Dr. Jacobi in *Sacred Books of East*, vol. XLV), p. 123.

royalty he became a *śramaṇa* and gained the *kevala-jñāna.* He became the twenty-third *tīrthaṅkara* and laid down the principle of the (*nirgrantha*) *śramaṇa* tradition. The word Jainism as we all know had not come in vogue for almost 1000 years after Lord Mahāvīra, who became the twenty-fourth and last *tīrthaṅkara,* modifying some of the principles laid down by Pārśvanātha. Varanasi is the second most important place after Ayodhyā in the old Jaina pantheon. Here were born three other *tīrthaṅkaras,* Supārśvanātha (at Varanasi), Śreyāṁśanātha (at Singhpuri or Sarnath) and Candraprabha at Candravatī, about 20 km from Varanasi on the bank of the Ganges on the eastern side, an area which is reckoned as part of Kāśī state.[6,7] Historical evidence may not support this tradition but about 22 other *tīrthaṅkara*s support it. Venerable Shamdung Rinpoche has said that everything cannot be tested on the touchstone of analytical historicity. He says that when footprints are made on freshly fallen snow they are there for a short while, and footprints vanish with more snowfall. It would be improper to say, therefore, that there were no footprints on the snow earlier. Passage of time obliterates them.[8] We are talking about an era when writing had not come in vogue, traditions and philosophical dogmas were all carried forward in the oral tradition. Why therefore should we have doubt about its truthfulness?

Reverting back to Varanasi once again we find that Varanasi is mentioned in the *Ṛṣibhāṣita* (third century BC), *Ācārāṅga* (second century BC), *Bhagavatī, Uttarādhyayana, Kalpasūtra* (first century BC), etc., and is associated with Pārśvanātha. Dr. Sagarmal states that in the Jaina Āgamas and *Kalpasūtra* Pārśvanātha is called Puruṣādānīya. In the *Aṅguttara Nikāya* also this word also comes and he is mentioned as the

6. Dr. Sagarmal Jain, *Jaina Paramparā meṅ Kāśī,* p. 278.
7. Dr. Moti Chandra, *Kāśī kā Itihāsa.*
8. Taranatha, *History of Buddhism in India,* 1968, p. 11.

son of King Aśvasena. Among other people connected with the times of Pārśvanātha are Āryadatta, his important disciple, Puṣpacūlā the chief *ārya*, and followers like Suvrata and Sunanda. Soma, his *gaṇadhara*, was the son of a brāhmaṇa of Kāśī and he was converted by Mahāvīra (*Antakṛta Daśāṅga*). His name also comes in the *Matsya Purāṇa*. Mahāvīra had come to Varanasi and his two disciples were Cūlanīpitā and Surādeva who were well-known businessmen of Kāśī. The *Uttarādhyayana* also gives the story of *cāṇḍāla* Harikeśa-Bala.[9]

Jainism had to fight it out with the ritualistic practices prevalent at Varanasi and this reminds one of the story of Kamaṭha (famous ascetic of *pañcāgni tapas*) and Pārśvanātha. This story is mentioned in the *Tīrthodgārikā* and *Āvaśyaka Niryukti*. In the *Uttarādhyayana-Sūtra* also are seen stories of such differences.[10]

Jainism has produced excellent *mūrti-kalā* iconography and historical records in its stone engravings. Apart from Khāravela inscription and Lohanipur torso, not much is available of this ancient period. However, it is surprising that while Kaṅkālī Ṭilā of Mathurā has produced superb works of Kuṣāṇa period, nothing has been found in Varanasi region till the end of Gupta period.[11] One important event mentioned of this period is that of the south Indian scholar Sāmantabhadra who composed the *Svayambhū-Stotra* and as per the story the four-faced image of Jinasvāmī Candraprabha emerged from a *Śivaliṅga*.[12] Absence of images and icons may be due to the absence of patrons in this period or the images got destroyed in the ruthless waves of invading armies' anger. We, however, are left with a few images from the seventh century to eleventh century which show that the Jaina community was still active

9. Dr. Sagarmal Jain, *Jaina Paramparā meṅ Kāśī*, p. 279.
10. *Ibid.*, p. 281.
11. *Ibid.*
12. *Ibid.*, p. 282.

in this period in Kāśī area. One copper plate inscription of Paharpur mentions about the Yāpanīya sect of Jainas (CE 479) who had a *vihāra* named Patagohali. This sect is now found only in the pages of history.[13] At the end of this period both Buddhism and Jainism had taken a severe beating from Ādi Śaṅkarācārya. While Buddhism became almost extinct, Jainism, which seemed to have migrated to western, central and south India survived but the cradle area of its origin, eastern U.P. and plains of Bihar seemed to have lost touch with Jainism.

Around CE 1194, when Muslim invaders devastated temples in Varanasi area it was a Jaina Seṭhiā (rich businessman) of Gujarat who sent one lakh gold coins for the restoration and reconstruction of Ādi Viśveśvara (Śaiva) temple of Varanasi.[14]

There is enough evidence to show that during the 600 years of Muslim rule Kāśī remained a pilgrim centre of Jainas who always stopped here on their way to Sammet-Śikhar in Bihar. In the *Vāstupāla Prabandha* mention has been made of restoration of Jaina temples in Varanasi by Tejpāla.[15] A lot of present-day images are of 15/17th century CE and manuscripts of this period are also available in Varanasi. The autobiographical book of poems — the first one in Hindi was by a Jaina scholar, Banarasi Das who mentions the social, religious and economic conditions of Varanasi and Agra area in his book *Ardha Kathānaka* (CE 1998).[16]

Varanasi, from time immemorial, had been reckoned as a centre of learning and people of various faith had come here to learn or propagate their views.

During this period it seems the *paṇḍits* of Varanasi were not freely giving away the knowledge available in Sanskrit

13. *Ibid.*
14. MM Pandit Gopinath Kaviraj, *Kāśī kī Sārasvata Sādhanā*, p. 2.
15. Dr. Sagarmal Jain, *Jaina Paramparā meṅ Kāśī*, p. 283.
16. Banarasi Dass, *Ardha Kathānaka*, Jaipur copy.

works to others. Despite this Yaśovijayajī, a Śvetāmbara monk of Gujarat came to Varanasi to study and after a few years he went back to Gujarat.[17]

He developed Navya-Nyāya in Jaina theology based on his studies here. Yaśovijaya is one of the four or five most important authors in Jaina philosophy. In the British period Bishop Hebber has mentioned about his visit to a Jaina temple in Varanasi.[18] With religious peace returning in the British era Varanasi once again developed into a centre of learning for Jainas also. Most of the notable Jaina scholars of the present times are the product of Varanasi. Mention has to be made of Syādvāda Vidyālaya and the important Pārśvanātha Vidyāpīṭha.

New temples coming up show the restoration of Varanasi as a *tīrtha* for Jainas also. One glaring omission in this narration is the effect of medieval *bhakti* movement of Jaina theology. The effect of *sakāma bhakti* and to some extent of Tantricism is to be witnessed in the worship of Padmāvatī. Some studies will be required to find out the rub-off of this movement and its philosophical content on the Jaina thought process.

17. MM. Pandit Gopinath Kaviraj, *Kāśī kī Sārasvata Sādhanā*, p. 79.
18. Dr. Moti Chandra, *Kāśī kā Itihāsa*, pp. 402-03.

2

Kāśī in Jaina Tradition

Sagarmal Jain

SINCE ancient times Kāśī has been holding an important place in the Jaina tradition. It has the pride of being the birthplace of four *tīrthaṅkaras*, namely Supārśva, Candraprabha, Śreyāṁśa and Pārśva. After Ayodhyā, Varanasi has the honour of being the birthplace of several *tīrthaṅkaras*. Supārśva and Pārśva were born in Varanasi; Candraprabha in Candrapurī, situated 15 km in the east of the Gaṅgā bank; and Supārśva in Siṁhapurī, the modern Sarnath.

Although three *tīrthaṅkaras* out of these four belong to pre-historical era, the historicity of Pārśva cannot be denied. He is mentioned in *Ṛsibhāṣita* (third century BC),[1] *Ācārāṅga* (second Śruta Skandha),[2] *Bhagavatī*,[3] *Uttarādhyayana*[4] and *Kalpa-Sūtra* (about first century BC).[5] In *Kalpa-Sūtra* and Jaina Āgamas he is called *puruṣādānīya*.[6] This word also appears in the *Aṅguttara Nikāya*[7] where he has been mentioned as the son of

---

1. *Ṛṣibhāṣita*, chapter 31.
2. *Ācārāṅga-Sūtra*, 2/15/245.
3. *Bhagavatī-Sūtra*, pp. 226, 378.
4. *Uttarādyayana-Sūtra*, 23/1.
5. *Kalpa-Sūtra*, 148.
6. *Ibid.*, 8.
7. *Aṅguttara Nikāya*, 7/290.

King Aśvasena and his period is accepted to be in the eighth-ninth century BC.[8] The identity of Aśvasena is borne by Haryaśva in the Purāṇas.[9] Several contemporaries of Pārśva are related with Varanasi. Āryadatta was his main disciple.[10] Puṣpacūlā was the chief Āryā,[11] several masters of the household[12] like Suvrata and several mistresses, like Sunandā[13] were his followers. Soma is mentioned as one of his prominent *gaṇadharas*. He was the son of an erudite brāhmaṇa of Kāśī[14] and finds mention in *Ṛṣibhāṣita*.[15] In the Jaina traditions Pārśvanātha has eight *gaṇas* and eight *gaṇadharas*.[16] Although Moti Chandra has made a mention of four *gaṇas* and four *gaṇadharas*, this is baseless.[17] The confrontation between Pārśva and Kamaṭha Tāpasa is mentioned in Jaina narratives.[18] The word *pāraśavaḥ* appears in the *Baudhāyana Dharmasūtra*, perhaps its relation was with the followers of Pārśva, although the original context is of *varṇa saṅkara*.[19] The *Jñātā-Dharma-Kathā* (first century BC) mentioned that the great daughters of Varanasi namely Ilā, Saterā, Saudāminī, Indrā, Dhannā, Vidyutā, etc., were initiated by Pārśva.[20] *Uttarādhyayana* also mentions about the initiation of Kāśirāja[21] who Kāśirāja is also mentioned in the *Mahāvagga* and *Mahābhārata*.[22]

8. *Kalpa-Sūtra*, 148.
9. Moti Chandra, *Kāśī kā Itihāsa*, p. 22.
10. *Kalpa-Sūtra*, 157.
11. *Ibid.*
12. *Ibid.*
13. *Ibid.*
14. *Ibid.*, 156.
15. *Ṛṣibhāṣita*, chapter 42.
16. *Kalpa-Sūtra*, 156
17. Moti Chandra, *Kāśī kā Itihāsa*, p. 38.
18. *Cauppannamhāpuriṣacarīyam*, 216.
19. *Baudhāyana Dharma-Sūtra*, 1/9/17/3.
20. *Jñātā-Dharma-Kathā*, 2/3/2-6.
21. *Uttarādhyayana-Sūtra*, 18/49.
22. *Antakṛtadaśāṅga*, 6/96.

The *Antakṛtadaśāṅga* mentions that Alakṣa Alarka, the king of Kāśī, was initiated by Mahāvīra.[23] Alarka has been mentioned as the king of Kāśī in the *Matsya Purāṇa*.[24] Though Śaṅkha, Kaṭaka and Dharmarūci have also been mentioned as the kings of Kāśī beside Alakṣa in the Jaina narratives, they have been said to belong to pre-Mahāvīra and Pārśva periods. It is, therefore, difficult to say about their historicity. Among the kings of Kāśī beside Alarka Alakṣa, Jitaśatru is also mentioned in the *Upāsakadaśāṅga* as contemporary of Mahāvīra.[25] But Jitaśatru is a title which is given to too many kings in the Jaina traditions. Therefore, it is difficult to deduce any historical conclusion on the basis of this name. It is presumed that among the ten main disciples of Mahāvīra, Culanīpitā and Surādeva were inhabitants of Varanasi. They were well-known businessmen. The *Upāsakadaśāṅga* gives a description of their opulence and devotion to *dharma*.[26] Mahāvīra himself visited Varanasi.[27] The characters of the chapters named Harikeśī and Yajñīya in *Uttarādhyayana* are also related to Varanasi.[28] In both, a strong dig has been made at casteism and ritualism. Jainism had to struggle a lot for its existence and enlightenment in Varanasi. In the present article we will discuss it briefly but before that it is essential to lay the geographical condition of Varanasi as described in the Jaina Āgamas.

---

23. *Matsya Purāṇa*, 180/68.
24. *Upāsakadaśāṅga*, 4/1.
25. *Ibid.*, 4/1.
26. *Āvaśyaka Niryukti*, 5/7 and *Upāśakadaśāṅga*, 4/1.
27. *Uttarādhyayana-Sūtra*, study 12 and 25.
28. *teṇaṁ kāleṇaṁ teṇaṁ samaeṇaṁ varanasi nāma nayarī hotthā, vannao* ।
tīseṇaṁ varanasie nayrīe bahiyā uttarapuracchie disibhāge ।
gaṅgāe mahānadīe mayaṅga tīraddahe nāmaṁ dahe hotthā ।
— *Jñātā-Dharma-Kathā*, 4/2

Kāśī is mentioned as a *janapada* (sector) and Varanasi as its capital in the Jaina Āgama *Prajñāpanā*. It is mentioned that the boundaries of Kāśī touch Vatsa in the west, Magadha in the east, Videha in the north and Kośala in the south. Kośala is mentioned in the north of Kāśī in the Bauddha scriptures. Gaṅgā is mentioned in the north-east of Varanasi in *Jñātā-Dharma-Kathā*. Location of Mṛta-Gaṅgātīrahṛda (pond) is also mentioned there.[29] It is a fact that Gaṅgā flows in the north-east near Varanasi at present, but its situation is not proved in any case in the north of Varanasi. There is only one alternative to prove this; and that is, if Varanasi is supposed to be on Rajaghat then Gaṅgā can be accepted in the north-east of the city. The word *mayaṅga* is described as Mṛta Gaṅgā in *Uttarādhyayana Cūrṇi* which implies that there was a stream of Gaṅgā that flowed in the north-east of the city, but it dried later. Its current did not flow and it took shape of a pond. Though Moti Chandra has informed about it but it still needs a strong proof. There is no mention of this dried stream of Gaṅgā in Jaina Āgamas and Cūrṇi. Since one form of Prākṛta word *mayaṅga* is also Mātaṅga, hence it could imply (on that basis) to be a closeby pond to the Gaṅgā bank. There is a mention in *Uttarādhyayana Niryukti* of the country of the Mātaṅgas (Śvapākas) near it.[30] Jaina Āgamas mention the gardens and forests namely Āśramapada (*Kalpasūtra*),[31] Koṣṭaka (*Upāsakadaśāṅga*),[32] Ambaśalavana (*Niryāvali*),[33] Kāmamahāvana (*Antakṛtadaśāṅga*)[34] and Tenduka (*Uttrā-dhyayana Niryukti*)[35] seated near Varanasi. *Aupapātika-Sūtra*

---

29. *Uttarādhyayana Niryukti*, study 12, p. 255.
30. *Kalpasūtra*, 153.
31. *Upāsakadśāṅga*, 3/124, *Āvaśyaka Niryukti*, 1302.
32. *Niryāvali*, 3/3.
33. *Antakṛtadaśāṅga*, 6/16.
34. *Uttarādhyayana Niryukti*, Study 12, p. 355.
35. *Aupapātika-Sūtra*, 74.

reveals many *tāpasa*s residing on the bank of the Gaṅgā, whose detailed account in this place is not required. But by this we get a view of the religious scenario of that era.[36]

Jaina Āgamas do not describe Varanasi as a city of Śiva. It was mentioned only in the fourteenth century in the *Vividha-Tīrtha-Kalpa*, while there are some old references about the tradition of worship of *yakṣa* here. The *Uttrādhyayana Niryukti* mentioned *yakṣāyatana* of Gaṇḍī Yakṣa in Tenduka Garden in the north-east of Varanasi. The same *yakṣa* was pleased with a Jaina *śramaṇa* Harikeśibala who was a *cāṇḍāla* by caste. This narrative is in detail in the *Uttarādhyayana Sūtras* and in their *Niryukti*s. The *śramaṇa* (ascetic) Harikeśibala goes to the place of offering for seeking alms. Being a *cāṇḍāla*, he could not get alms from the place of offering and was driven out after a good beating. The *yakṣa* becomes angry. All seek his forgiveness. Harikeśa elucidates the true form of *yajña*, etc.[37]

From the present account it can be derived that the opposition against *yakṣa* worship in the *śramaṇa* tradition was not that strong as it was against the sacrificial *yajña*. This new spiritual interpretation of *yajña* of *Uttarādhyayana* is mentioned in *Mahābhārata*. It is perhaps due to this incident of Harikeśa that the Gaṇḍī Yakṣa of Varanasi came to be known as Harikeśa Yakṣa. In *Matsya Purāṇa*, there is a narration of Harikeśa Yakṣa and he is mentioned as a man of pure nature and austerity but he has been described as Śiva-*bhakta*.[38] The narrative of *Uttarādhyayana* is older than the narrative of *Matsya Purāṇa*. The source of the narrative is the same, which has been transformed in accordance to the respective religious perspectives. In the context of *yakṣa* worship Dr. Moti Chandra has mentioned

36. *Uttarādhyayana-Sūtra*, study 12.
37. *Matsya Purāṇa*, 180/6-20 and 180/88-99, *Uddhṛta Kāśī kā Itihāsa*, p. 33.
38. *Kāśī kā Itihāsa*, Moti Chandra, pp. 32-33.

two events — 3/14 and 16/16 — of *Uttarādhyayana*. But both are confusing.[39] The description of *cāṇḍāla śramaṇa* of Harikeśibala and his helping *yakṣa* is in the 12th chapter of *Uttarādhyayana*. Gaṇḍitinduka *yakṣa* is mentioned by name in the *Uttarādhyayana Niryukti*.[40]

Jainism has always been opposing ritual practices and casteism and such three incidents of resistance are related to Varanasi. In the first incident there is a struggle between Pārśvanātha and Kamaṭha Tāpasa. The second incident relates to the struggle of Harikeśibala against *yājñika*s in which there is condemnation of casteism and violent *yajña*s. The third was the struggle between Jayaghoṣa and Vijayaghoṣa. It also describes a man of pure conduct as a true brāhmaṇa and the *varṇa* system is mentioned as being related with deeds, not birth.

These struggles have been mentioned in Jainism from the time of Pārśva. In fact, these were mainly aimed against the ritualistic traditions. As it is well known, Jainism has always opposed ritualistic practices, its main emphasis has been on internal purity, self-control and wisdom. Pārśvanātha is believed to be the son of Varanasi's king, Aśvasena. Pārśva in his childhood had to struggle against those *tāpasa*s who believed that torturing the body is the height of religiousness and who in their ignorance propagated such belief in the name of religion. Kamaṭha was well-known as *tāpasa* during the time of Pārśvanātha. He used to perform *pañcāgni tapa* (penances with five fires). In his *tapa* or penance of fire, various creatures were sacrificed either intentionally or out of ignorance. Pārśva had tried to convince him that only the ritualistic practices did not constitute *dharma*, rather the discrimination and self-control are its requisites. At the same time there is no scope for body torturing in self-discipline. Pārśva opposed blind

39. *Uttarādhyayana Niryukti*, study 12, p. 355.
40. *Tīrthodgārika*.

faith and ritualistic practices in the field of religion. Thus we find that Varanasi was the centre where Jainism had to struggle first for its foundation. The confrontation between Pārśvanātha and Kamaṭha has been mentioned in *Tīrthodgārika*[41] and *Āvaśyaka Niryukti*[42] in Jaina literature. In fact, the conflict between Pārśvanātha and Kamaṭha is the conflict between the path of knowledge and the body-torturing ritualism. The conflict between the followers of Pārśvanātha and Kamaṭha also figures in *Baudhāyana-Dharma-Sūtra*. The second struggle between Jainism and Brahmanism has been mentioned in *Uttrādhyayana Sūtra*. Actually, this struggle aimed at the opposition of casteism or the brāhmaṇa superiority. *Uttrādhyayana* and its *Niryukti* inform us that Varanasi was the central place of the conflicts between Harikeśibala and Rudradeva as well as between Jayaghoṣa and Vijayaghoṣa.[43] This narration is available in Āgama *grantha*s and their *niryukti*s and *cūrṇi*s, and furnishes information about the presence of Jainism in Varanasi in the era before Christ.

The position of Jainism in Gupta's period in Varanasi is still a matter of investigation. Possibly some facts may come to light from *bhāṣya* and *cūrṇi*s. The archaeological proofs, the image of Ṛṣabhadeva received from Rajaghata and one copper-plate of Gupta Saṁvat 158 (CE 479) received from Pahārpur are some of the evidences which indicates the inhabitation of Jains in Varanasi in those times. This copper plate gives information about the existence of a Jina temple called Paṭagohālī Vihāra in Varanasi.

Administration of this *vihāra* was in the hands of the disciples of Ācārya Guṇanandī [44] who was a *śramaṇa* of Pañcastūpānvaya, a sect of Yāpanīya, different from

---

41. *Tīrthodgārika*.
42. *Āvaśyaka Niryukti*.
43. *Āvaśyaka Niryukti*.
44. *Uttarādhyayana-Sūtra*, study 12 and 25.

Śvetāmbara and Digambara traditions. The copper plate indicates that there was an influence of the Yāpanīyas in Varanasi too as it was in Mathura.

Another incident of Gupta period relates to Jaina Ācārya Samantabhadra. It appears that the influence of Brahmanism was most dominating in the Gupta period in Varanasi. According to the unwritten Jaina accounts, Ācārya Samantabhadra was a scholar of fourth-fifth century in Jainism. He was suffering from *bhasmaka* and for this he travelled to Varanasi from south India. According to the oral Jaina accounts, he performed the duty of a priest in a Śiva temple and he used to satiate himself with the offerings. Once he was caught eating the offerings and so in order to protect his honour, according to the narrative, he composed the *Svayambhū-Stotra*, the impact of which resulted in the emergence of the four-faced image of Candraprabha from *Śivaliṅga*.

Though the narrative is only traditionally related, from this a few things can be derived. First, Samantabhadra had to come to Varanasi for quenching thirst for knowledge from other philosophical systems, because Varanasi was considered as a centre of learning in those times. His acceptance of the duty of a priest in a Śiva temple perhaps signifies that either it was impossible for him to learn the Vedic traditions as a Jaina *muni* or the country of the Jaina inhabitants had become so insignificant that to earn his livelihood he had to perform the duties of a priest. It was perhaps the aim of attaining knowledge which led him to become a priest because a brāhmaṇa could not agree to impart knowledge to a Jaina *muni* who did not believe in God. In this way the Jainas had to struggle for acquiring knowledge in Varanasi. As has been mentioned earlier, the Jainas were in existence in Kāśī even during the Gupta period. However, it is difficult to say that how much and to what extent the Jainas were influential in Varanasi during that period. Archaeological evidences indicate only about the existence of Jaina temples here. Among the few Jaina images found in Kāśī, the image of Mahāvīra of about sixth century CE, is significant. This image is kept in Bharat Kala Bhawan (No. 162). The image of Nemināṭha, found in Rajaghata, is also supposed to belong to the seventh century and this is also kept in Bharat Kala Bhawan. The image of Ajitnātha and the image of Pārśvanātha which belong to the seventh and eighth centuries respectively were also discovered in Varanasi and are at present kept in the State Museum, Lucknow. These discoveries indicate that the Jaina images and temples were in existence in Varanasi during the fifth-sixth centuries to the eighth-ninth centuries. This establishes the fact that there was inhabitance of Jainas in Varanasi in those periods.

The Jaina archaeological remains of the ninth, tenth and eleventh centuries have also been found from Varanasi. An image of Vimalanātha belonging to the ninth century has been preserved in the Sarnath Museum (No. 236). Again an image of Ṛṣabhanātha belonging to the tenth century and the head of the image of the *tīrthaṅkara* belonging to the eleventh century have been discovered. These images are also kept in Bharat Kala Bhawan (No. 176 and 197). The time of these images has been established by Dr. Maruti Nandan Prasad Tiwari in his writing *Jaina Dharma and Art in Kāśī.*[45] We have presented this time-scheme on the basis of those writings. We also get information about Varanasi during the twelfth, thirteenth and fourteenth centuires in *Prabandhakoṣa* and *Vividha-Tīrtha-Kalpa*. The descriptions of Govind Candra, the king of Kāśī, his sons Vijaya Candra, etc.,[46] are met with in *Harṣakavi Prabandha* of *Prabandha Koṣa*. Tejapāla Vastupāla has even mentioned the renovations of Jina-temples of Varanasi.[47]

45. Moti Chandra, *Kāśī kā Itihāsa*, p. 100.
46. Dr. Vidyadhar Joharapurkar, *Vīr śāsan ke Prabhāvaka Ācārya*, p. 33.
47. Dr. Maruti Nandan Tivari, *Kāśi Men Jaina Dharma evaṁ Kalā.*

Among the descriptions of Varanasi in the *Vividha-Tīrtha-Kalpa,* most are the narratives of the Āgama era. But the author of the *Vividha-Tīrtha-Kalpa* had also added the narrative of Hariścandra in it. This scripture gives us two or three pieces of information about Varanasi in the fourteenth century.[48] Firstly, it was famous as a seat of learning and secondly it abounded with scholars and brāhmaṇas. The author of the *Vividha-Tīrtha-Kalpa* has given us an important information about Varanasi that the city was divided into four parts in those periods: Deva Varanasi where the temple of Viśvanātha was located and the worship of *jinacaturviṁśati paṭṭa* was in practice. The second was the kingdom Varanasi which was inhabited by Yavanas. The third was Madana Varanasi and the fourth was Vijaya Varanasi. Along with this he has mentioned the *caitya* of Pārśvanātha, *dharmekṣā stūpa* of Sarnath and Candraprabha in Candravatī. At that time the monkeys used to jump here and there, animals roamed and the demons or fiends wandered openly in Varanasi.[49] Such description made by Jinaprabha appears to be an open eye account of Varanasi. Even today the Deva Varanasi can be connected with the nearby area of Viśvanātha temple. Shri Moti Chandra has stated about the Varanasi kingdom's relations with the area of Adampura and Jaitpura. He has assumed Madana Varanasi to be in Jamaniyā tehsil of Gazipur and Vijaya Varanasi to be in Vijayagaḍh of Mirzapur, but in my opinion Madana Varanasi and Vijaya Varanasi should be parts of Benaras (Varanasi). Was not Madana Varanasi the Madanpura of modern times? Similarly, was not Vijaya Varanasi situated nearby modern Bhelupur. I hope that scholars will investigate further and provide information.

We get evidence of both types, archaeological and literary, about the situation of the Jainas in Varanasi in the fifteenth,

---

48. *Prabandha Kośa — Harṣakavi Prabandha.*
49. *Ibid., Vastupāla Prabandha.*

sixteenth and seventeenth centuries. Firstly, several images in the temples are present and these belong to that era. Secondly, many hand-written texts of those periods are also available in the Jaina collections. Thirdly, we find some hints about Varanasi of those periods in *Ardhakathānaka* of Banārasīdāsa who originally belonged to Agra, stayed at Benaras for a long time, in connection with his vocation and he has also described it in his autobiography *Ardhakathānaka*. According to his description, Nabāḅ Kilach Khān, Sūbedār of Jaunpur, had put all the jewellers of that place behind the bars in 1598. He has narrated in detail about Benaras in sixteenth century in *Ardhakathānaka*.[50] This book is published.

In the seventeenth-century Śvetāmbara *muni*, Upādhyāya Yaśovijaya of Gujarat, visited Benaras for learning. Varanasi has always been a centre of learning and Jaina scholars visited from time to time for learning religious philosophy (*dharma-darśana*s). However, it is also the matter of consideration that they had to face many difficulties in this connection. Jaina images and hand-written texts belonging to the sixteenth, seventeenth and eighteenth centuries are available in Varanasi although there is scarcity of detailed searchings.[51]

In the first half of the nineteenth century there was adequate number of Jainas in Varanasi. Bishop Hebar records many mutual disputes of Jainas of that time. Generally, the entry of others was banned in the Jaina temples. Bishop Hebar was given permission to enter the Jaina temple alongwith Prinsep and Mekaliyada. He has given a detailed account of his visit to the Jaina temple, his meeting with the Jain *guru* and the welcome he had received (*Kāśī Kā Itihāsa*, Moti Chandra, pp. 402-03).[52]

---

50. *Vividha-Tīrtha-Kalpa*, Varanasi Kalpa.
51. *Ibid.*
52. Moti Chandra, *Ardhakathānaka Uddhṛta Kāśī kā Itihāsa*, p. 210.

The Jaina *ācārya*s tried to convert this city of learning into the centre for study of Jainism in the end of the nineteenth century and in the early decades of the twentieth century. Since the brāhmaṇa teachers generally did not want to impart their knowledge to Jaina, hence there were only two alternatives before them — either to attain the knowledge of other religious philosophies in disguise or to establish an independent centre for the learning of Jainism. Gaṇeśa Varṇī and Vijaya Dharmasūri made determination to independently open schools for learning of Jainism here. As a result, Yaśovijaya School in Angreji Kothi and Syadvad College in Bhadaini were founded. While Yaśovijaya School produced Jaina scholars of Śvetāmbara tradition like Pandit Sukhalalaji Sanghvi, Pandit Bechardas, etc., Syadvad College, on the other hand, brought forth scholars of Digambara tradition, like Pandit Kailasa Canderji Shastri, etc. Most of the present scholars of the Digambara tradition are the products of Syadvad College. Although, Yaśovijaya School could not survive for a long time, yet one of the many scholars who were products of this college, was Pandit Sukhalalaji who held the post of teacher of Jaina philosophy in the Banaras Hindu University and gave birth to Pārśvanātha Vidyāśrama by his inspiration, which is a prominent centre of higher study of Jaina philosophy in Varanasi at present.

Thus, Jainism had been in existence continuously in Varanasi from the period of Pārśvanātha to the modern times which is a long duration of about 28 centuries and this city has made a great contribution in the advancement of Jainism and its arts.

3

Tīrthaṅkaras of Kāśī

B.S. Mehta

MENTION has been made about four *tīrthaṅkara*s, several Jaina temples and about the scholars who had come from different places in Kāśī. The 7th, 8th, 11th and 23rd *tīrthaṅkara*s were born in Kāśī. This phenomenon has added to the glory (*kāśyatā*) of Kāsī, thereby acquiring potentiality to face Brahmanic and Buddhist *śramaṇa* culture.

The twenty-four *tīrthaṅkara*s have been worshipped in Jainism. Who are these *tīrthaṅkara*s? I have been able to know about them from two texts. The first being the *Cauvīśī* of Ānandadhana and the second, *Dhanānanda and Ānandadhana,* a book of Acarya Vishvanath Prasad Mishra. A common Hindi reader does not discriminate between *Dhanānanda* and *Ānandadhana* as he believes that both are the names of a single poet. The great *ācārya* elucidated in his much investigated preface that one of them was "Ānanda" who wrote a book on music called, *Rāga Kalpadruma.* Ananda Kāyatha belonged to the family of poet Ānanda of Koṭa Hisār. His period is traced to the third part of the seventeenth century. Another poet was Ānandadhana who was also a "Kāyastha" but he was the Mīr Munśī of Muhammad Śāha Raṅgīlā, the emperor of Delhi. Perhaps he had composed the book, *Koka Mañjarī.* It is said that he went to Vrindavan in the last part of his life and was killed in the attack by Nādir Śāha. The third Ānandadhana was a contemporary of Yaśovijaya, who was a Jaina and his original name was Mahātmā Lābhānanda. He also lived in the second half of the seventeenth century VS. He composed his *Cauvīśī* in CE 1621. Ānandadhana of Bṛja was a contemporary of Nāgarīdāsa. The fourth Dhanānanda is very prominent. He was one of the prominent poets of *rītikāla* in Hindi literature. He was a romantic poet writing *kavitta* and *savaiyyā*. He is different from poet Ānandadhana of Vrindavan, because his *Padāvalī* (literary composition), emotional touches and language are totally different from that of the *kavitta* of Dhanānanda. Bharatendu Babu Harishchandra had made a collection of the poems of Dhanānanda in *Sujāna Śataka*. Alongwith Dhanānanda, the poet of love, Ānandadhana, the *bhakti* poet and Ānanda the musician, the fourth one Ānandadhana was a Jaina poet. His three books *Aṣṭa-Padī*, *Cauvīśī* and *Bahottarī* are in Gujarati and his several memoirs are available. Ānandadhana is the one who is under critical study in the present essay.

There are *stavana*s (worshipful eulogies) of 24 *tīrthaṅkaras* in his *Cauvīśī*. Out of these 24 *stavana*s, 22 are composed by Ānandadhana and the remaining two are by Jñāna Vikāya and Jñāna Sāri. There are more than 100 *pada*s (stanzas) in his second book *Bahottarī*. Among them several *pada*s are composed by Sūra, Kabīra, devotional poet Ānandadhana, Jaina poet Banārasī Dāsa and Dayāvata. It is difficult to find out *pada*s of an original poet but from it we get an inkling of the poet's nature. Acharya Kshiti Mohan Sen has called him a mystic poet, but if we go deeper into the matter we find that it contains Jaina spiritualism, which is the foundation of his spiritual thinking. *Aṣṭa-padī* is printed in Gurjar literary collections.

We are acquainted with their *avadāna*s through these *stavanas*. Apart from these four *tīrthaṅkaras*, the first *tīrthaṅkara* Ṛṣabhadeva and the 24th *tīrthaṅkara* Mahāvīra Svāmī also have had connection with Kāśī. Similarly, in the list of prominent persons in Jainism, the ninth Cakravartī Padma and the twelfth Cakravartī Brahmadatta have been connected with Kāśī.

A brief introduction of *stavanas*, of *Cauvīśī*, and prominent persons, the *tīrthaṅkaras*, who are pride of Kāśī, is being given below:

1. The first *tīrthaṅkara* is Ṛṣabhadeva. During his period *svayaṁvara* of Sulocanā was performed. According to the *Cauvīśī*, Ṛṣabhadevajī distinguished between worldly love, marital love, and true love:

   prīta sagāi re jagamāṁ sahu kare, re prīta sagāi na koya ।
   prīta sagāi re nirupādhika kahā re sopādhika dhana khoya ॥

   Ṛṣabhadeva does not consider world a *līlā* (play) of God:

   koi kahe līlā re alakha alakha taṇī re lakha pūre manāsa ।
   doṣarahita ne līlā navi dhare re, līlā doṣa vilāsa ॥

2. The 7th *tīrthaṅkara* Supārśvanātha took birth in Kāśī and attained the four *kalyāṇakas* — pre-natal state, birth, penance and wisdom here only. He was born in the present Bhadaini Mohalla or Bhadravānī or Bhadrāvanī in old Kāśī. His father was Pratiṣṭhita, a king in Ikṣvāku lineage and mother Pṛthivīṣeṇā. Supārśvanātha ruled in the Kāśī kingdom for a long time and after that he attained the knowledge of salvation or pure knowledge (*kaivalya*) by penance. He attained *nirvāṇa* on Sammed Śikhara. His *stavanas* in *Cauvīśī* are composed in *rāga sāraṅga*, *malhāra* and *lalavānī*. His *avadānas* are notable. The first is to remove seven dreads, which are the following:

   Worldly fear, fear of after life, fear giving, accidental fear, occupational fear, fear of infame, fear of death.

   It is written:

   śrī sāta mahābhaya ṭālato, saptama jinavara deva ।
   sāvadhāna manasā karī, dhāro jina para seva ॥

Ānandadhana called God by 15 names in this *stavana*: Śiva, Śaṅkara, Jagadīśvara, Cidānanda, Bhagavān, Jina, Arihant, Tīrthaṅkara, Jyotisvarūpa, Asamāna, Alakha, Nirañjana, Vatsala, Sakala Jantu Viśrāma and Abhayadānadātā Pūrṇa Ātmārāma.

Supārśvanātha also gave aphorisms and thoughts, based on experiences which are — *vītarāga* (conqueror of desires), *vītabhaya* (conqueror of fears), *vītarati* (conqueror of passionate love), *vītarāga* (conqueror of desirelessness), *vītaśoka* (conqueror of sorrows), *vinidrā* (conqueror of sleep), *vītandrā* (conqueror of ennui), *vītadurdaśā* (conqueror of bad situations), *kalpanārahita* (freedom of imaginings), *abādhita yogī* (hurdleless *yogī*), *parama puruṣa* (superman), *parmātmā* (God), *parmeśvara* (God of gods), *pradhāna* (supermost), *parama padārtha* (super material), *parameṣṭhi* (superior deity), *parama deva* (super god), *pramāṇa* (evidence), *vidhi* (mode), *virañci*, *viśvambhara* (pervader), *ṛṣikeśa*, *jagannātha* (lord of the world), *aghahara*, *aghamocana*, *dhaṇī* (the Lord), *mukti* (salvation), *paramapada* (the highest state of existence).

3. The eighth *tīrthaṅkara* is Candraprabha. He took birth at Candrāvatī or Candrapurī in Varanasi *janapada* (sector). This place is situated on the bank of the Gaṅgā beyond Sarnath. His father Mahāsena was a king of Ikṣvāku lineage and his mother's name was Queen Lakṣmaṇā. He also attained four *kalyāṇakas* — pre-birth state, birth, penance and wisdom in Kāśī. He attained *nirvāṇa* (salvation) on "Sammed Śikhara." His *stavana* in *Cauvīśī* is composed in *rāga kedārā*, *gaurī* and *deśī*. Ānandadhana said:

candraprabha mukhacandra sakhī mune dekhaṇa de
mukha cāṅda ।
upasama (śānta) rasano kanda, sakhīgata kālamala dukha
dvandva ॥

His learning is:

nirmala sādhu bhagati lahī, yoga avañcaka hoya ।
kriyā avañcaka tima sahī, phala avañcaka soya ॥

4. The ninth prominent person Padma glorified Kāśī by declaring it as capital of India.
5. The eleventh *tīrthaṅkara* is Śreyāṁśanātha — was born in Siṁhapurī (Sarnath). Viṣṇu, a Kāśī king of the Ikṣvāku lineage was his father and Queen Nandā his mother. He was born on the 11th day of the dark fortnight in the month of Phālguna. A temple at his birthplace close to the Dhamekha Stūpa is in existence. Śvetāmbara temple is situated close to Hīrāmanpur village near Sarnath. His *stavana* is composed in *rāga gauḍī* and *deśī* in *Cauvīśī*. Ānandadhana said:

   śrī śreyāṁsanātha jina antarayāmī, ātama rāmī nāmī re ।
   adhyātmā pada pūraṇa pāyī, mahaja sugati gatirāmī re ॥

   Śrī Śreyāṁśanātha called the worldly people as given to senses and *munis* as *ātmārāmīs* (staying in spirit); *ātmārāmīs* are selfless. In the *stavanas* there is commentary on spiritualism of Śreyāṁśanātha:

   nija svarūpa je kiriyā sādhe, te adhyātma lahiye re ।
   je kiriyā kari caugati sādhe te, tena adhyātma kahiye re ॥

   Here *caugati* implies *deva* (god), *manuja* (man), *tiryaka* and *nārakī*. Attaining values of the self by *nīma*, *ṭhavaṇa*, *dravya* (materialism), *bhāva* (emotions) in spiritualism is totally useless. Those who respect *nirvikalpa* (thoughtless) by understanding the meaning of spiritualism are nice people, the rest are idlers.

   vastu jate je vastu prakāśe, ānanda dhana matavāsī re ।

6. The 12th prominent personage is Cakravartī Brahmadatta. He was a resident of Kāśī and his mention is made in several scriptures.

7. The 23rd *tīrthaṅkara* Pārśvanātha — after a long time a historical personality, founder of *śramaṇa dharma*, Pārśvanātha was born at Bhelupur Mohalla in Kāśī, in 800 BC on the 11th day of the dark fortnight of Pauṣa month. Aśvasena of Uaraga lineage, king Kāśī, was his father and Queen Vāmādevī, his mother. His birth is a milestone in the history of the city. He was initiated at a young age. He opposed anarchism, violence and torturing of body in the name of *dharma*. It is said that a *tāpasa* named Kamaṭha was performing *pañcāgni tapa* (penance of the five fires) and an *ajñāna mūlaka yajña* (nescience-destroying *yajña*). A pair of male and female snake was burnt in the fire of *yajña* but Pārśvanātha saved them. They became famous by the name of Indra and Indrāṇī, Dharaṇendra Deva and Padmāvatī in their next birth and were called *yakṣa* and *yakṣiṇī* in their own reign.

   The narrative has its own place, perhaps the beginning of the snake worship all over India, especially worship of *yakṣa* in Kāśī, is linked with their reign. Worship of *yakṣa* is a symbol of unlimited devotion of people for Bhagavān Pārśvanātha. The symbol of snake and the images having seven fangs of the snakes have become recognition of Pārśvanātha.

   His *stavana*s are in *sāraṅga rāga* in *Cauvīśī*:

   dhruvapada rāmī ho svāmī, māharā niḥkāmī guṇarāya sujñānī ।
   nijaguṇa kamī ho pāmī tūṅ dhaṇī, dhruva ārāmī ho thāya ॥

   and

   śrī pārasa jina pārasa rasa samopiṇa ihāṅ pārasa nāhi ।
   pūraṇa rasīyo ho nija guṇa parasano ānandadhana mujha māṁhi ॥

Another *stavana* is in *rāga deśī*:

ātama dharama anusārī rame je ātama rāma re ।
ānanda dhana padavī lahe, parama ātama tasa nāma re ॥

Pārśvanātha founded *cāturyāma dharma*. These *yāma* were — 1. Non-violence, 2. Truthfulness, 3. Non-stealing (*acaurya*), 4. Non-possession.

Gaining knowledge of salvation (*kevala jñāna*) after twelve years of penance, the 24th *tīrthaṅkara* Mahāvīra, initiated in Śramaṇa *dharma*, added another canon (*yāma*) to this — that was of celibacy (*brahmacarya*). And thus was *pañca-mahāvrata* founded.

8. The 24th *tīrthaṅkara* Mahāvīra — According to the Jaina accounts Jitaśatru, a king of Kāśī, used to worship Mahāvīra Svāmī. He paid visits to Koṣṭhaka *caitya* out of Varanasi several times. Mahāvīra initiated another king of Varanasi named Lakṣa, in the *caitya* of the village Mahāvana. One more king of Kāśī named Śaṅkha was initiated by Mahāvīra.

   Similarly, Koṭyādhīśa Seṭh Culanīpitā and a rich householder Surādeva are counted among the prominent disciples of Mahāvīra.

The one main motto of Mahāvīra is — "Non-violence is the highest religious duty (*ahiṁsā paramo dharmaḥ*)."

The basic principles of Jainism are — Syādvāda and Anekāntavāda. Along with these, the thought of Saṁvarā and Nirjarā in the convictions of actions (*karma*) is remarkable.

Ānandadhana has written in *Cauvīśī* in his *stavana* — *vīra jine caraṇa lāgūṅ vīra paṇute māṅgū re*. He was named Mahāvīra (a great conqueror) because he did not conquer others but his own self.

4

Nativity and Marks of Tīrthaṅkaras and Varanasi's Contribution

P.C. Jain "Premi"

FROM the first *tīrthaṅkara* R̥ṣabhadeva to the last *tīrthaṅkara*, Mahāvīra, there has been a long tradition of twenty-four *tīrthaṅkaras* in the Jaina *dharma*. Their names respective marks and birthplaces are as under:

S. No.	*Name*	*Marks*	*Birthplace*
1.	R̥ṣabhadeva	Ox	Ayodhyā
2.	Ajitnātha	Elephant	Ayodhyā
3.	Sambhavanātha	Horse	Śrāvastī
4.	Abhinandana	Monkey	Ayodhyā
5.	Sumatinātha	*Cakavā* (a large orange-brown duck)	Ayodhyā
6.	Padmaprabha	Lotus	Kauśāmbī
7.	Supārśvanātha	*Svastika*	Varanasi
8.	Candraprabha	Moon	Candrapurī (Candravatī, Varanasi)
9.	Puṣpadanta	Crocodile	Kākandī (modern Khukhandu, district Deva-riya (U.P.))

10.	Śītalanātha	Kalpavṛkṣa (desire fulfilling tree)	Bhaddilapura Bhadrikapur modern Bhondalagaon; in Hajaribagh district (8 km from Kolhua hills)
11.	Śreyāṁśanātha	Rhinoceros	Sinhapur (Sarnath)
12.	Vāsupūjya	He-buffalo	Campāpurī (Bihar)
13.	Vimalanātha	Hog (wild boar)	Kāmpila
14.	Anantanātha	Sehi	Ayodhyā
15.	Dharmanātha	Bajradaṇḍa (rod)	Ratnapurī
16.	Śāntinātha	Antelope	Hastināpura
17.	Kunthunātha	He-goat	Hastināpura
18.	Arahanātha	Fish	Hastināpura
19.	Mallinātha	Pitcher (pot)	Mithilā
20.	Muni Suvratanātha	Tortoise	Rājagṛha
21.	Naminātha	Blue lotus	Mithilā
22.	Neminātha	*Śaṅkha* (conch-shell)	Śaurīpur
23.	Pārśvanātha	Snake	Varanasi
24.	Mahāvīra	Lion	Vaiśālī Kuṇḍagrāma

Since the images of all the *tīrthaṅkara*s are in the *padmāsana* (lotus posture) or *kāyotsarga* (standing in penance) with equal half-closed eyes, absorbed in meditation, these images can be recognized by their distinguishing marks which are engraved in the middle front of the back foot of the images. Although, the images of these *tīrthaṅkara*s can be recognized by their distinct *yakṣa* and *yakṣiṇī* their symbols are the prominent means of recognition. Some *tīrthaṅkara*s can be recognized even by the characteristics of different symbols.

The birthplaces of four out of 24 *tīrthaṅkaras* happen to be in Varanasi. Among these four *tīrthaṅkaras* the first is the seventh *tīrthaṅkara*, Supārśvanātha who was born in Jainaghata situated on the banks of the Gaṅgā in Bhadaini Mohalla. The second is the eighth *tīrthaṅkara* Candraprabha whose birthplace is the village Candrāvatī situated about 25 km from Benaras on the banks of the Gangā. The third is the 11th *tīrthaṅkara* Śreyāṁśanātha whose birthplace is Sarnath, the famous tourist place. The fourth is the 23rd *tīrthaṅkara* Pārśvanātha. His birthplace is Mohalla Bhelupur, situated in the middle of the Benaras city, where three splendid Jina temples are embellished. The auspicious personality and the unique characteristics of the four *tīrthaṅkaras* born in Benaras are described below:

Tīrthaṅkara Supārśvanātha (*fig.* 1)

In the tradition of twenty-four *tīrthaṅkaras* in Jainaism, the seventh *tīrthaṅkara* Supārśvanātha took birth in Bhadrāvanī, modern Bhadaina Mohalla in Varanasi city in Kasi kingdom. He was born in the palace of the king Supratiṣṭhita, located on the banks of the river Gaṅgā. He was in the Ikṣvāku lineage and Queen Pṛthvīṣeṇā was his mother. Supārśvanātha was born on the twelfth day of the bright half of the month Jyeṣṭha, in an auspicious *yoga* called Agnimitra, many millenniums ago. Three magnificent Jaina temples (two Digambara and one Śvetāmbara) erected in the memory of his birthplace can be still seen on the banks of the river Gaṅgā. Śrī Syādvāda College has also been running since last nine-ten decades under Śrī Supārśvanātha Jinālaya, situated at Jaina-ghata. More than hundred scholars of this college are dedicated to the service of Jaina *dharma*, philosophy and culture. The four *kalyāṇakas* — pre-natal state, birth, penance and wisdom, were also attained by *tīrthaṅkara* Supārśvanāth in Varanasi.

There are five kinds of knowledge in Jainism — intelligence (*mati*), knowledge gained through hearing (*śruta*), extant (*avadhi*), peace of mind (*manaḥ paryaya*) and pure knowledge (*kevala jñāna*). In his childhood Supārśvanātha was so talented that he had attained the first three of the aforesaid knowledges before birth. Notwithstanding the ample means of joy and pleasure around him, he remained indifferent to them. He even got married and had able sons just to follow the family traditions. He succeeded his father and proved himself a worthy king. Even so, his mind remained occupied always with the aim of self-attainment. One day on seeing a change of season, he realized the ephemeral nature of the universe. After such realization he handed over his kingdom to his son and on the twelfth day's evening in Viśākhā *nakṣatra* in the bright half of the Jyeṣṭha month he went to Sahetuka forest along with one thousand kings. He gave up his royal dress and adornments for ever and got initiated and restrained himself like a *muni*. He attained the knowledge of peace of mind (*manaḥ paryaya jñāna*) just after initiation.

On the second day after initiation when he came out for alms ceremoniously, Mahendradatta, the king of Somakheta kingdom was blessed for offering food. His restraint was growing continuously and it was aimed at self-goodness as well as the welfare of the creatures of the world.

For the attainment of the highest knowledge all the vows and fasts together with devout meditation and spiritual excercises (*sādhanā*) became a part and parcel of his life. The people were motivated and astonished and used to say that being a popular king of a vast kingdom he took no time in giving up delusion of the kingdom and throne. Now what an incomparable firmness of continuous penance is on the way of restraint? Thus after a firm penance of nine years when he was absorbed in meditation under *śirīṣa* tree, he attained *kevala jñāna* in Viśākhā star on the seventh day of the bright half of Phālguna month. People became overjoyed. The god Indra and all human beings celebrated the festival of the *kevala jñāna kalyāṇaka* (highest) with great enthusiasm. In this one can attain, through supra-sensuous self-sufficiency, a total knowledge of all the three phases of the times — past, present and future and also the knowledge of the entire material abundances along with its possible substitutes of the three worlds.

According to Jainisim an ascetic on attaining *kevala jñāna* attains the place of supreme virtue (*parameṣṭhi*) namely, *arhant* which is first among the five supreme virtues (*parameṣṭhī*s) and becomes omniscient. So after this self-attainment the *tīrthaṅkara bhagavān* Supārśvanātha, inspired and motivated by the strong will of welfare of all the creatures of the world, started delivering discourses through religious assembly, namely *samavasaraṇa*. In this *samavasaraṇa* all the creatures — men, gods, *tiryañc*, etc., listen to the divine voice of *bhagavān* altogether.

Visiting almost all the prominent kingdoms like Kāśī, Kośala, Mathurā, Magadha, etc., *tīrthaṅkara* Supārśvanātha started to deliver spiritual discourses. While his own spiritual exercises (*sādhanā*) were still going on, gradually the people too who were desirous of attaining *mokṣa* joined him and took initiation. Thus was formed a vast sect. Thousands of *munis*, *āryikā*, *śrāvaka*s and *śrāvikā*s became his followers. He had 95 *gaṇadharas*. For a long time he visited every part of India and its border areas and firmly influenced people to follow the path of truth and non-violence. His influence was powerful and all-pervading. In the last month of his life-span he dwelled at the Sammed hill-top in Bihar State where he assumed *pratimāyoga* and attained *nirvāṇa* in the Viśākhā *nakṣatra* on the seventh day of the dark half of Phālguna month. His *nirvāṇa* festival had been celebrated in a grand manner by the people and the gods all together. *Tīrthaṅkara* Supārśvanātha's popularity and all-pervading influence are evident from the fact that, through his enlightening preachings and by other utilitarian tasks for the welfare of all the creatures of the world, he has been able to make his place in the heart of the people. His splendid images are embellished in the Jina temples situated in every part of the country. His mark is *svastika*. But his old images are combined with the fangs of snakes also which are similar to the images of Pārśvanātha. The difference between the two is only that while in the images of Pārśvanātha the number of fangs is usually seven or more, the number of fangs in the images of Suparśvanātha is five. The auspicious mark of *svastika* is his permanent distinguishing mark along which his images are also seen engraved with a *yakṣa* named Varanandin and a *yakṣiṇī* named Kālī. In some cases the name of the *yakṣa* is found to be Vijaya and the *yakṣinī* Puruṣadattā.

Archaeological Proofs of Worldly Influence

His vast influence had been in the Śaurasena region, especially in the Mathura area. The remains of a *stūpa* discovered at the famous Kankali Tila of Mathura are its proof. Ācārya Jinaprabhā Sūri has mentioned about it in his book, *Vividhatīrthakalpa,* that this *stūpa* of gold was made by Kuberā Devī in the period of Supārśvanātha upon which an image of Supārśvanātha was fixed. Later, in the period of Pārśvanātha, it was covered with bricks. Bappabhaṭṭa Sūri renovated it in the eighth century.[1] Ācārya Somdeva Sūri, the writer of *Yaśastilaka Campu,* had visited this *stūpa* and has made a mention that it has been made by gods. In the narrative of Vajra Kumāra, in *Hariṣeṇa Kathākoṣa,* there is a mention of this *stūpa* to have been made by Vidhyādharas for Vajra Kumar. According to the renowned poet Rājamalla, the composer of *Jambūsvamī Carita,* this *stūpa* had also been renovated by Sahu Todar. The poet himself had visited this *stūpa*. According to him, there were 514 *stūpa*s at that time. Another proof of the aforesaid *stūpa* of *bhagavān* Supārśvanātha is the image discovered at Kankali Tila. In a write-up about this image it has been mentioned that this *stūpa* was made by gods. This

1. Pandit Balbhadra Jaina, *Ancient History of Jain Dharma,* first part, p. 129, Keśarīcandra Jaina, 1974.

tablet of homage of Kusāṇa period is also considered important in support of this viewpoint.

Thus, the *tīrthaṅkara* Supārśvanātha was an influential and utilitarian *tīrthaṅkara* of his times. Ācārya Samantabhadra of the third century has thus praised him in the following words:

> *sarvasya tattvasya bhavān pramātā, māteva bālasya hitānuśāstā,*
> *guṇāvalokasya janasya netā mayāpi bhaktyā pariṇūyate'dya* ॥5॥
>
> O Supārśva Jina! you are the creator of all the elements. Like a mother you deliver discourses to the ignorant and to the child. You are the protagonist of those who are in search of virtues. That is why I am praying to you with devotion.

The Eighth Tīrthaṅkara, Candraprabha (*fig.* 2)

In the tradition of twenty-four *tīrthaṅkaras* the eighth *tīrthaṅkara,* Candraprabha, took birth in Candrapura, modern Candrāvatī on the banks of the Gaṅgā in Varanasi Janapada in Śukrayoga on the eleventh day of the dark half of Pauṣa month. His father, Mahāsena of Kāśyapa *gotra,* was a king of Ikṣvāku lineage and his mother's name was queen Lakṣmaṇā. He had the knowledge of understanding (*mati*), knowledge gained through hearing (*śruta*) and extant knowldege (*avadhi jñāna*) since his birth. Following the traditions he had succeeded the throne after his father. Despite his following all the worldly traditions of marriage, getting sons, administration of the State and the enjoyment of all sorts of pleasures, he remained detached and secluded from within. Once while looking himself in the mirror in his dressing room, he noticed the apparent effect of his advancing of age on his face and thus erupted his inner feeling of renunciation. Having realized the ephemeral nature of the universe, the body and the happiness, he became indifferent to them. He thought "What is the use of such joy which does not spring from the soul? What is the use of that wealth which is transitory? What is the use of the youth that withers? What is the use of that age which is time-bound? Although we all know about what has happened in this world and what will happen in the future yet we are ensnared by delusion again and again; and this is really surprising." Thus bewildered at the transitoriness of everything, he developed a desire of renouncing the world. He handed over his kingdom to his son Varacandra and on the eleventh day of the dark half of Pauṣa month under the auspicious star, Anurādhā, he went to Sarvartuka forest alongwith many kings where he performed *pañcamuṣṭi keśaluñca* (taking out the hair from the roots in Jaina tradition) and got initiated in Jaina tradition.[2] He attained the knowledge of peace of mind (*manaḥ-paryaya-jñāna*) as soon as he took initiation. The people had celebrated the festival of his initiation (*dīkṣā kalyāṇaka mahotsava*) with great enthusiasm.

After two days of initiation he had gone to Nalin city for meals, where king Somadatta was blessed for offering food to *munirāja* Candraprabha with nine-fold devotions (*navadhā bhakti*).

Immersed in self-spiritual excercises *munirāja* Candraprabha used to carry out five superior religious rites as non-violence, etc., five fold (*samiti*) — *īryā*, *bhāṣā* (language), *eṣaṇā* (desires), *ādāna nikṣepaṇa* and *pratiṣṭhāpana*, ten *dharma*s restraining five senses, supreme forgiveness, *mārdava*, *ārjava*, etc., and the other basic virtues and later developed virtues of *śramaṇa*s. Penance, *dhyāna*, *yoga* were also being practised uninterruptedly. Finally, in the evening of the seventh day of the dark half of the Phālguna month in Anurādhā *nakṣatra*, he gave a deadly blow to the destructive deeds — coverings of knowledge, coverings

---

2. *kiṁ sukhaṁ yadi na svasmātkā lakṣmīścendriya calā* ।
kiṁ yauvanaṁ yadi dhvaṁsi kimāyuryadi sāvadhi ॥45.205 ॥
tatraṁ kiṁ jātama pyeṣ yatkāle kiṁ vā bhaviṣyati ।
iti jānannahaṁ cāsminmomuhībhi muhurmuhuḥ ॥45.208 ॥
etyayenāyate naivamāyāsita evākulaḥ ।
kālalabdhiṁ pariprāpya kṣuṇṇamārga jihāsayā ॥45.211 ॥
— Ācārya Guṇabhadra *viracita Uttara Purāṇa*

of vision, delusion and obstructions (*antarāya*) — and got himself accessed in *kṣapaka* category, and attained the *Sayogakevalī Guṇasthāna.* His spirit had become gnostic and rich with unlimited knowledge, happiness and energy. He had secured five attainments: *paramāvagāḍh samyagdarśana* (equal vision), *yathākhyāta cāritra, kṣāyika jñāna,* etc.

With this he had become omniscient and had attained the place of supreme virtue (*parameṣṭhi*) namely *arhant*. People had celebrated the festival of *Jñāna Kalyāṇaka* on the occasion of his attaining *kevala jñāna,* the supreme knowledge. At the same time, all the creatures could for the first time listen to his divine discourses through *samavasaraṇa* and got themselves blessed. Thus, he promoted *dharmacakra*. Svāmī Samantabhadra had mentioned about him in *Svayambhū-Stotra*.

> *yaḥ sarvaloke parameṣṭhitāyāḥ padaṁ babhūvādbhutakarma-tejāḥ* ।
>
> *anantadhāmākṣara viśvacakṣuḥ samantaduḥkhakṣayaśāsanaśca* ॥
>
> He who has attained the place of supreme virtue (*parameṣṭhi*) in the whole universe, he who has attained the divine energy of the rites, he who has attained the infinite energetic immortal vision of the world (*kevala jñāna*) and whose instruction has the power of destroying all kinds of sorrows — such Candraprabha Jinendra should purify my mind.

He had a vast sect of *śramaṇa*s in which beside 63 *gaṇadhara*s like Datta there were many *munis, āryika*s and *śrāvaka*s and *śrāvikā*s, endowed with the vast knowledge and spiritual power (*ṛddhi*).

He also had visited every part of the country counselling the people to follow the path of *dharma*. Finally, assuming *pratimāyoga,* he had dwelled on the Candraprabha hills (*ṭoṅk*) on Sammed Śikhara near Pārasanātha in Hajārībāga district (Jharkhand) for a month and had attained the highest place of *mokṣa* (*nirvāṇa*) in Jyeṣṭhā *nakṣatra* on the seventh day of the dark half of Phālguna month after having prevented the *yoga* and having completely destroyed the remaining four *aghātiyā karmas*: *vedanīya, āyu, nāma* and *gotra*. The people had celebrated the occasion of his *nirvāṇa* (*mokṣa*) *kalyāṇaka* with great delight.

His image can be recognized by the mark of the moon engraved in the middle of the back foot. The name of his *yakṣa* and *yakṣiṇī* are Vijaya or Śyāma and Jvālāmālinī respectively.

At present, at his birthplace Candrāvatī village situated near Varanasi, there are two Jaina temples on the pleasant banks of the river Gaṅgā. Among them, one is related to the Digambara and the other to the Śvetāmbara Jaina traditions. Here he had attained the four *kalyāṇakas*: pre-natal state, birth, penance and wisdom. Candrāvatī has also been known as Candrānana and Candramādhava. Many ancient remains of archaeological significance are still being found in the surrounding areas of Jaina temples on the banks of the river Gaṅgā. An old deep well used to exist until a few years back. A notice board, regarding its protection has also been fixed by the Archaeological department. From the presence of these ancient remains, it can be supposed that further excavations will provide us with more proofs of the ancient city and more remains of the Jaina temples and images. Ancient Jaina temples are in danger as there has always been a continuous erosion of the banks of the river Gaṅgā. Hence, it needs to be protected beforehand.

On studying the scripture *Vividhatīrthakalpa,* written by Ācārya Jinaprabha Sūri in the fourteenth century, we have come to know that Sūri had visited Candrāvatī and he has mentioned it as a prosperous pilgrimage centre. Praying to *tīrthaṅkara* Candraprabha, Svāmī Samantabhadrācārya said:

> *candraprabhaṁ candramarīcigauraṁ candraṁ dvitīyaṁn jagatīva kāntam* ।
> *vande'abhivandyaṁ mahatāmṛṣīndraṁjinaṁ jitasvāntakaṣāya bandham* ॥

Possessed of fair-complexion like beams of the moon, delightful as the second moon in the world, praised by the higher souls, lords of the initiated *munis*, conqueror of the enemies of *karmas* and conqueror of his inner *kaṣāyabandhana* is *bhagavān* Candraprabha. I pray to him.

Tīrthaṅkara Śreyāṁsanātha (*fig.* 3)

Praying to Bhagavān Śreyāṁsanātha, Svāmī Samantabhadra said:

śreyān! jinaḥ śreyasi vartmanīmāḥ śreyaḥ prajā śāsadajeya vākyaḥ ।
bhavānścakāśe bhuvanatraye 'sminneko yathā vītaghano vivasvān ॥

O Śreyāṁsanātha Bhagavān! a conqueror of the enemies of *karmas* and connected with the unobstructed speeches, delivering spiritual discourses to the people about the virtues of *mokṣa,* you are shining alone in the three worlds like the sun not covered by the clouds.

Such eleventh *tīrthaṅkara* Śreyāṁsanātha took birth in Sinhapur (Sarnath) city near Varanasi on the eleventh day of the dark half of the Phālguna month in Viṣṇuyoga at the abode of his father King Viṣṇu of Ikṣvāku lineage and his mother queen Nandā.

He had the three kinds of knowledge — knowledge of intelligence (*mati*), knowledge gained through hearing (*śruta*) and extant (*avadhi*) — since his birth. He reached his adolescence, making his people and the family happy by his efficiency, brilliance and compassion. He married at young age and became an able successor of his father. Under his regime the kingdom enjoyed the highest goal of prosperity and peace, which indicates that he was an efficient and kind-hearted king.

In *Uttara Purāṇa* (57-40-41) Ācārya Guṇabhadra has mentioned about the characteristics of his personality:

Śreyāṁsanātha Mahārāj had developed himself energetic like a precious stone, sober like an ocean, cool like the moon

> and philanthropic like *dharma,* working life-long for the welfare of the people and skillful in *śāstras*. He had got all sorts of abundances as a reward for his auspicious deeds done in the past birth. Hence his wisdom and vigour were confined only to the *dharma* and the virtuous deeds.

Like this he ruled for forty-two years. At last the time had come when his spiritual practices of many births came into effect. In the spring season, during the occasion of *Ānandotsava,* he noticed the sudden change in season and such realization caused the asceticism lying dormant as a seed in his mind to erupt. He began brooding about the time and felt that when the time which overpowers the world is itself not perpetual as it ceases with the change of moment, minutes and hours; then how can there be stability in other materials. Truly, the whole world is prone to destruction. Only the state of *mokṣa* is perennial. How can a person attain everlasting joys without having attained *mokṣa*? So I should strive only for the attainment of *mokṣa*.

After such logical reasoning he got the acceptance from his people for the initiation and thus after handing over his prosperous kingdom to his able son Śreyaskara he went to Manohar garden in the morning of the eleventh day of the dark half of the Phālguna month under the Śravaṇā *nakṣatra*. He gave up the royal dresses and adornments, and did *pañcamuṣṭi keśaluñcana* (pulled out hair) and restrained himself like a *muni*. He attained the knowledge namely peace of mind (*manaḥ-paryaya-jñāna*) just after the initiation.

On the second day after initiation he got alms as a *muni* at the palace of king Nanda in Siddhārtha Nagar. After two years of penance in the same beautiful garden he attained *kevala jñāna* while performing fast for two days under the *tumbūra* tree in the evening on the *amāvasayā* (new moon) of the Phālguna month under Śravaṇā *nakṣatra.* All the gods and human beings together celebrated the festival of *Jaina Kalyāṇaka*. Thenceforth, he delivered discourse for the first time in divine religious assembly (*samavasaraṇa*) and all the creatures got benefited from his divine voice. Thus started his *dharma* persuasion.

He had a vast sect (*śramaṇa saṅgha*) consisting of seventy-seven *gaṇadharas* like Kunthu, and several wise *munis, āryikas, śrāvakas* and *śrāvikās* as *Caturvidha śramaṇa saṅgha* were his followers. He visited many countries and regions along with his *saṅgha,* blessing salvation to the creatures through his divine voice, and finally reached the Sammed Śikhara. Here he stopped practising *yoga* for a month and assumed *pratimāyoga*. He destroyed a series of uncountable effects of the remaining deeds (*karmas*) on the full moon night of the month of Śravaṇā by the last two bright meditations (*śukla dhyānas*) in a duration in which five small letters — अ (a), इ (i), उ (u), ऋ (ṛ), ऌ (lṛ), can be pronounced and then after attained *nirvāṇa*. The people together celebrated the occasion of his *Mokṣa Kalyāṇaka* with great enthusiasm.

His images are marked by rhinoceros for its recognition. Along with it, there had also been a tradition of combining the images with the carving of *yakṣa* named Īśvara, and *yakṣiṇī* named Gaurī. A Digambara Jaina temple at his birthplace Saranath, close to the Dhameka *stūpa* is in existence in a vast area in which many old images are also installed. Here he had attained the four *kalyāṇakas* — pre-birth state, birth, penance and wisdom. An old Śvetāmbara Jaina temple can also be seen in Hiramanapur village (Sinhapur) near Sarnath station. It was founded by Jinakuśala Candrasūri in *VS* 1657.

The twenty-third Tīrthaṅkara Pārśvanātha (*fig.* 4)

In the glorious tradition of 24 *tīrthaṅkaras*, the personality of the 23rd *tīrthaṅkara* Pārśvanātha whose birthplace is Benaras, has been very much influential and has been worshipped as the most popular idol and the lord removing all obstacles and difficulties of life. The early literature of the Jaina traditions which is available in modern times is directly related to the

24th *tīrthaṅkara* Vardhamāna Mahāvīra, but before him was the *tīrthaṅkara* Pārśvanātha who was born in Kāśī in the ninth century BC. Aśvasena, the king of Kāśī was his father and queen Vāmādevī was his mother. He was a great dignity in this *śramaṇa* tradition. Although, about him no systematic literature is available in modern times, many old historical evidential sources proved him a historical dignitary.

Pārśvanātha took birth in Ugra lineage. In the *Baudhha Jātakas,* there is a mention of the names of the ancestors of Brahmadutta, the king of Varanasi — Uggasena, Dhanañjaya, Mahāsolava, Saṁyama, Vissasena and Udayabhaṭṭa. Perhaps Ugra lineage came into vogue from Uggasena. In the *Bṛhadāraṇyaka,* in the dialogue between Gārgī and Yājñavalkya, Gārgī has said "Kāśyo" or "Vaideho" or "son of Ugra" (*kāśyo va vaideho ugraputraḥ*). This implies that people of Kāśī and Videha are the sons of Ugra. Among the aforesaid names mentioned in *Bauddha Jātakas* the name of "Vissasena" is of much importance because in Prākṛta literature the second name of Aśvasena, the father of Pārśvanātha, has been mentioned as "Vissasena" (Viśvasena). People of Ugra lineage, etc., also belonged to the Ikṣvāku lineage.

According to a narration in Purāṇas, Pārśvanātha's mother Vāmādevī, before his birth had seen sixteen auspicious dreams in the last *prahara* (a three hour's period) of the night which signified that Pārśvanātha had come in the womb of his mother. So on the second day of the dark half of the month of Vaiśākha under Viśākhā *nakṣatra,* the mother held the soul Ānatendra of the past world of Pārśvanātha which came from Ananta heaven in her auspicious womb, and since then she had become energetic like the eastern rays. After nine months, on the 11th day of the dark half of the Pauṣa month under *anila yoga* and Viśākhā star, she delivered the child who later became famous as *tīrthaṅkara* Pārśvanātha. He remained bachelor till the age of 30 years. After that he got himself initiated as a *muni* along with three hundred kings on the

11th day's morning of the dark half of Pauṣa month. He had to face many terrible difficulties on the ways of restraints and meditation, but he remained immersed in the penance, without getting disturbed. After a long series of religious practices he had attained the highest *kevala jñāna* on the fourth day of the dark half of the month of Caitra. He had also attained the status *arhant* and thus became omniscient.

After self-attainment he visited all the places like Kāśī, Kośala, Pāñcāla Marahaṭā, Māru, Magadha, Avantī, Aṅga-Baṅga-Kaliṅga, etc., for the sake of the welfare of the people. He had spread the message of non-violence, truth, etc., through his religious discourses. He had advised people to give up the disorders like the religious blindness, showiness, feeling of class-distinction, etc. Visiting everywhere he had reached the Sammed Śikhara near Hazaribagh. Here he had attained *mokṣa* (*nirvāṇa*) in the morning of the seventh day of the bright half of Śravaṇā month just after his assuming of the *pratimāyoga* and destroying the remaining *aghātī* deeds (*karma*s). Thus, for the well-being of the people he visited all over the country. The popularity of his noble life and religious philosophy can be seen all over India and its neighbouring countries and regions as well in various manners even today. His images are mainly recognized by the seven fangs of snake and by the mark of a snake in the middle of the back foot. His several images comprising thousand fangs and more are also in existence. The engravings of the *yakṣa* Dharaṇendra and the *yakṣiṇī* Padmāvatīalso help in recognizing his image.

Popularity and Influence

In Ardhamāgadhī Prākṛta literature he has been mentioned as a much popular personality and has been given several honorific titles such as "Puruṣādāṇīya" meaning Lokanāyaka, (admired by the people), the superior person. The deep impression of his thoughts and influence on many religions like the Vaidika, the Bauddha and the Indian culture of non-violence and spiritualism is apparent even today. His mention in the Vaidika, Jaina and Bauddha literature and therein the mention of the castes like Vrātya, Paṇi, Nāga clearly indicates that they were the followers of Pārśvanātha. The snake worship in modern India also seems to be related with him.

According to the *Ancient History of Jaina Dharma* (part I, p. 356), *tīrthaṅkara* Pārśvanātha was undoubtedly honoured by the castes Nāga and Draviḍa. The caste Nāga was the most powerful among the Vrātyas who were the followers of the *śramaṇa* culture. Takṣaśilā, Udyānapurī, Ahicchatra, Mathurā, Padmāvatī, Kantipurī, Nagapur, etc., were famous centres of Nāga caste. *Tīrthaṅkara* Pārśvanātha had visited the centres of the Nāga race several times. Influenced by his deep thoughts the Nāgas became his followers. A detailed study and a deep investigation in this context can provide surprising and new facts which can more distinctly describe the all-pervading personality of *tīrthaṅkara* Pārśvanātha.

In this context the statement of Professor Jagadisha Gupta of Allahabad University, holds importance, which is as under:

> Significance of *tīrthaṅkara* Pārśvanātha is supported by the worship of *nāga*, cobras, *yakṣa* and sun. It proves how much popular was he in the Indian culture and in how many forms he has been portrayed and engraved. With how much zeal the Indian artists have enriched his forms with the power of their imagination. How many forms of snake-umbrella are found — this can be recognized by a deep study of countless images of Pārśvanātha. In my opinion, in order to understand the true colour of Indian culture if any Jaina *tīrthaṅkara* is important after *tīrthaṅkara* Mahāvīra and Gautam Buddha, in the viewpoint of art then that is Pārśvanātha.[3]

---

3. *Contribution of Jaina Dharma in Indian Culture and Literature*, p. 26 quoted from his article collected in the book, Akhil Bhartiya Digambar Jaina Vidvatparisad, 1996.

The famous Jaina king of Kaliṅga, Mahārajā Khāravela of the second century BC was also one of his prominent followers. In Āgamas mention has been made of many regions, nations and countries of that time which Pārśvanātha had visited along with his *saṅgha* and had spread awareness among the people through his religious discourses. These regions, nations and countries are Aṅga, Baṅga, Kaliṅga, Kuru, Kośala, Kaśī, Avantī, Puṇḍra, Mālava, Pāñcāla, Magadha, Bhadra, Daśārṇa, Saurāṣṭra, Karnatak, Koṅkaṇ, Mevār, Lāṭ, Kashmir, Kaccha, Vats, Pallava, Āmīr, etc.

In the eastern parts of India, especially in the tribal (*ādivasī*) areas of many States like Bengal, Bihar, Orissa, etc., the tribes like Sarāka, Sadagopa, Raṅgiyā have a close affinity with the tradition of *tīrthaṅkara* Pārśvanātha. The deep impression of the *tīrthaṅkara* Pārśvanātha and his thoughts as well are clearly evident in their daily routine and *saṁskāras*. All the Sarākas and several people of the non-Jaina castes worship Pārśvanātha as their family god and a favoured deity till today.

Thus, *tīrthaṅkara* Pārśvanātha and his popular thoughts have had deep impressions on the religious, social, cultural and spiritual fields for a long time. His religion was easy to follow from the viewpoint of customary practices. During his times the practice of the violent and ignorant penances for having sons, wealth and the world, etc., were in vogue. Hence, Pārśvanātha had visited the aforesaid areas and had spread the powerful doctrines of non-violence, which had influenced the society deeply, and many of the Ārya and Anārya castes took initiation in his *dharma*. The adoption of the non-violent means in the places where violence in the name of *dharma* was prevailing, has been possible because of the great impact of the spiritual discourses of Pārśvanātha.

The penance of the five fires (*pañcāgni tapa*) performed by Kamaṭha on the banks of the river Gaṅgā in Kāśī and the protection of a pair of male and female snakes which were being burnt in the fire of *yajña* by *ṇamokāra mantra* when he was a prince, and the conversion of those male and female snakes into *yakṣa* Dharaṇendra and *yakṣiṇī* Padmāvatī; are some of the incidents which are symbolic of the establishment of non-violence and discrimination by him and his opposition to violence and the nescient (*ajñāna mūlaka*) ritual practices which were prevalent in the field of religion. Praying to him Ācārya Samantabhadra said:

> *ya satya vidyātapasāṁ praṇāyakaḥ samagradhīrugrakulām-baraṁśumān* ।
>
> *mayā sadā pārśvajinaḥ praṇamyate vilīna mithyāpatha dṛṣti vibhramaḥ* ॥
>
> You are the founder of the true education and penances, you are omniscient and teacher of complete wisdom. You are like the moon in the sky of Ugra lineage. You have eradicated the false visions and many wrong viewpoints and have thus founded the path of balanced sight (*samyag darśana*), supreme knowledge and noble character. So Pārśva Jin! I always pray to you for these virtues.

The presence of the images of *tīrthaṅkara* Pārśvanātha in the thousands of old and new Jaina temples in our country is mainly due to the deep devotion and faith in him and his strong and all-pervading influence on the public. The Vrātya kṣatriyas of the middle and the eastern countries were his followers. People of the adjoining areas of the river Gaṅgā and its southern parts, and the kingdoms and republics of the Nāga lineage, were his followers. The dialogue "Kāśī Gautam" included in the 23rd chapter of *Uttarādhyayana* is quite famous. This *śramaṇa* of Śrāvastī was also in the tradition of Pārśva. The whole royal family were his worshippers. Parents of *tīrthaṅkara* Mahāvīra and his relatives were *śramaṇa* worshippers of Pārśvāpatya tradition.[4]

---

4. *Upadeśamālā Gāthā*, 92.

There is a mention of *śrāvaka* named Vappaśākya of *nirgranthas* in Pāli literature, who was the paternal father of the Lord Buddha.[5] This makes clear that the paternal lineage of *bhagavān* Buddha was Pārśvapatyīya. It is necessary to clarify here that the word Pāsāvaccijja, that is to say Pārśvapatyīya and Pāsattha (Pārśvastha), have been used in Ardhamāgadhī Āgamas in reference to the followers of Pārśvanātha. It means — the tradition of Pārśva or the *śramaṇa* and the worshipper *śramaṇa* following his tradition.

A few references also establish that *bhagavān* Buddha was initially initiated in the *nirgrantha* tradition of *bhagavān* Pārśva. But later on he made his own sect.

We have come to know in the context of Mahātmā Buddha's life that he must have been related to Pārśva tradition in his state of *sādhanā*. According to a mention of *Majjhima Nikāya*, Mahāsiṁhanādasutta (1.1.2) once said to his disciple Sāriputra:

> Sāriputra! before the attainment of perfect knowledge (*bodhi*) I used to pluck out hair of beard and moustache. I used to perform penance in the standing and sitting postures. I lived naked. I never used to perform worldly practices. I used to take alms on palm and eat it. If ever the food was offered to me on the place where I was sitting or if the food was particularly cooked for me or if any invitation for taking food was there, I never used to accept it. I did not accept alms from pregnant lady and the lady who was feeding a baby from her breasts.

Such mode of living mentioned by the Buddha is also of Jaina ascetics. It signifies that Gautama Buddha was initiated in *śramaṇa saṅgha* and he had attained a lot of knowledge from there. Later on for some reason he became aloof, adopted the middle path and had established his own doctrine.

5. Pāli *Aṅguttara Nikāya*, Catuṣkhanipat, Mahāvaggovappasutta, 4-20-5.

Jaina *ācārya* of the eighth century has also mentioned that in the beginning Gautama Buddha was initiated as a Jaina *muni*. He said,

> The *śramaṇa* namely Pihitāśrava had also taken initiation in the *saṅgha* of Pārśvanātha on the banks of the river Sarayū in village Palāśa and he was named Muni Buddhakīrti. After some time he began to take fish meat and put on red clothes and started delivering discourses of his new *dharma*.[6]

Even if some scholars do not consider significance of this mention from the viewpoint of historicity but due to this mention of compatibility to the aforesaid *Majjhima-Nikāya* we cannot ignore this mention of Devasenācārya.

There is a mention of the doctrines of six *tīrthaṅkara*s of Makkhali Gauśālaka sect in *Sāmññaphalasutta* of Pāli *Dīgha-Nikāya*, among which the mention like *cāturmāsa saṁvara* (period of four months in which the Jaina *muni*s dwell at one place) as to say Sabbavārivāritta, Sabbavāriyutto, Sabbavāridhutto and Sabbavāriphuto with the name of Nigganṭha Nātaputta, had not been seen by me in any Jaina *śāstras*.

Some historians have also considered that after the prominent Vedas, *yajña-yāga*, etc., in the incorporation of the main spiritualistic thoughts in the Upaniṣads there has also been a lot of influence of the thoughts of *tīrthaṅkara* Pārśvanātha. Thus, his valuable contribution in reforming the spiritual form to the Vaidika tradition can be considered.

Thus, it can be said that *tīrthaṅkara* Pārśvanātha had such a magnetic personality and thoughts that any person who had come in his contact or in the association of his tradition would become his devoted follower. For just that reason the prominent

---

6. *siripāsaṇāhatitthe sarayūtīre palāsaṇayarattho* ।
pihiyāsavassa sisso mahāsudo baḍḍhaditti muṇī ॥
. . . . *stabaraṁ dharittā pavaṭṭiaya teṇa eyattaṁ* ।
— *Darśanasāra Gāthā* 6-8

personality of the Hindi world, Bharatendu Harishchandra has written:

> *tumahi tau pārśvanātha ho piyāre* ।
> *talaphana lāgai prāna bagala tai chinahu hota na nyāre* ।
> *tuma sau aura pāsa nahi kou mānahu kari patiyāre* ।
> *'harīcandra' khojata tumahī ko veda-purāna pukārai* ॥

Thus just as for Hindus and for the followers of other *dharma*s Kāśī is a holy pilgrimage, in the same way it is an ancient holy pilgrimage for the followers of Jaina *dharma* also. Since this land has been sacred with four *tīrthaṅkara*s' four *kalyāṇaka*s each — pre-birth state, birth, initiation and wisdom — out of five *kalyāṇaka*s, the unlimited reverential belief of the followers of the Jaina *dharma* of the entire country with this pilgrimage is only natural. For this reason lakhs of people visit this great pilgrimage centre every year for praising and worshipping and thus realizing their life's goal. The discovery of many Jaina remains and images belonging up to the third century, which are of archaeological significance, also support the aforesaid conceptions. Apart from these, the land of Kāśī has been regularly visited by many other *tīrthaṅkara*s.

5

Significance of Sarnath in Jaina Tradition and Art

S.S. Sinha

KĀŚĪ has been well known since ancient times for acquisition of *dharma*, literature and knowledge; it has been a place where all the Indian religions have developed. The ancientness of the Jaina *dharma* has been proved by the literary and the archaeological evidences. From the point of view of Jaina *dharma* also, Kāśī has been famous as a pilgrimage, a place of *sādhanā* and attainment of knowledge since ancient times. Varanasi has been described in different Jaina scriptures; such as *Prajñāpanā*, *Jñātā-Dharma-Kathā*, *Uttarādhyayana Cūrṇi*, *Kalpasūtra*, *Upāsaka-daśāṅga*, *Āvaśyaka Niryukti*, *Nirayāvalikā*, *Antakṛtadaśāṅga*,[1] *Tiloyapaṇṇatti* (written by Yativṛṣabha), *Uttara Purāṇa* (written by Guṇabhadra) *Pārśvanātha Caritra* (penned by Vādirāj Sūri) and *Ārādhanā Kathā Koṣa* (written by Nemidatta).[2] Besides, Varanasi has been mentioned in detail in *Vividhatīrthakalpa*, in which while introducing Varanasi it has been divided into four parts namely, Deva Varanasi, Viśvanātha Prāsāda, Madana

---

1. Satyendra Mohan Jaina, *Digambar Jaina*, Śrī Pārśvanātha Janmabhūmi Mandir, Bhelupur, *Historical Introduction of Varanasi*, Varanasi, 1995, p. 3; Moti Chandra, *History of Varanasi*, Varanasi, 1985.
2. Balbhadra Jaina, *Digambara Jaina Pilgrimage of India*, vol. 1, Bombay, 1974, pp. 111-34.

Varanasi and Vijaya Varanasi. Viśvanātha Prāsāda has been also called the capital of Varanasi.[3]

Sarnath has also been a part of Kāśī. As an archaeological proof Jagat Singh, a *dīvān* (Prime Minister) of the king of Kasi, had received all of a sudden the *Bauddha Mañjūṣā* from Sarnath which had drawn attention of the people. As a result an excavation work started at Sarnath. A lot of remains of art related to Buddha and to Hindu and Jaina religion as well, was discovered after this excavation which have further added to the importance of this place in the perspective of Indian art and culture. Most of the antiquities related to Buddhism have been found at Sarnath, among which the most primitive is the pillar combined with images of lion-heads the third century BC. The remains belonging to the periods of Kuṣāṇa, Gupta and Gahadavala have also been found here. Among these there are *stūpa*s and world famous images of Buddha (especially the images in the posture of *dharma-cakra-pravartana*).

The twenty-four *tīrthaṅkara*s have been honoured as super gods (gods of gods) in Jaina *dharma*. These *tīrthaṅkara*s are eternal symbols of the basic perception of sacrifice and *sādhanā* (worship) of Jaina *dharma*, which are the basic foundations of Jaina *dharma*. In the family of Jaina gods, the other gods are generally imagined to be related to these *tīrthaṅkara*s or as being their companions.

The twenty-four *tīrthaṅkara*s of the present Avasarpiṇī era are Ṛṣabhanātha, Ajitnātha, Sambhavanātha, Abhinandana, Sumatinātha, Padmaprabha, Suvidhinātha (Puṣpadanta) Śītalanātha, Śreyāṁśanātha, Vāsupūjya, Vimalanātha, Anantanātha, Dharmanātha, Śāntinātha, Amaranātha, Mallinātha (Mallinātha is mentioned as female *tīrthaṅkara* in Śvetāmbara tradition), Munisuvrata, Neminātha, Pārśvanātha and

3. Jinprabhasūri *Vividhatīrthakalpa*, ed. Jinvijaya, Sindhī Jaina Granthamālā, Granthāṅka 10, Shanti Niketan, Bengal, 1934, p. 74.

Mahāvīra (Vardhamāna).[4]

Among the twenty-four *tīrthaṅkaras*, the four *tīrthaṅkaras* have attained different *kalyāṇaka* (pre-birth state, birth, initiation and wisdom) in Varanasi. For this reason Varanasi has been of specific significance in Jaina *dharma*. The 7th *tīrthaṅkara* Supārśvanātha and the 23rd *tīrthaṅkara* Pārśvanātha were born in Varanasi at the modern Bhadaini and Bhelupur respectively, whereas the 8th *tīrthaṅkara* Candraprabha took birth at Candrapurī, about 23 km from Varanasi. According to Ācārya Jinaprabhasūri of the fourteenth century, the distance between Varanasi and Candrapurī was two and half *yojana* which is equal to the aforesaid distance.[5] Jinaprabhasūri has also made a mention of another fact that Candraprabha Svāmī also had attained four *kalyāṇakas* here.[6] It has been mentioned that the 11th *tīrthaṅkara* Śreyāṁśanātha was born at Siṁhapurī which has been recognized as modern Sarnath.[7] Since it is a birthplace of Śreyāṁśanātha it has a particular significance in Jaina tradition even today.

Varanasi has been holding an important place in Jaina tradition since Gupta period. The antiquities received from Rajaghata and from different places of Varanasi are its evidence. These antiquities have been preserved in the Bharat Kala Bhavan (Varanasi), the Archaeological Museum (Sarnath) and the Government Museum (Lucknow, U.P.). The references related to the *kalyāṇakas* of four *tīrthaṅkaras* of Varanasi, namely, Supārśvanātha, Candraprabha, Śreyāṁśanātha and Pārśvanātha have been mentioned in the scripture *Tiloyapaññati* written by Yativṛṣabha which are as under:

4. Maruti Nandan Tiwari, *Jaina Pratimā Vijñāna*, Varanasi Science of Jaina Images, 1981, pp. 30-31.
5. Lalit Chandra Jaina, *Vārāṇasī Jaina Tīrtha Darśana*, Varanasi, 1997, p. 15.
6. *Vividhatīrthakalpa*, p. 74.
7. Kamal Giri, Maruti Nandan Tiwari and Vijay Prakash, *Temple and Images of Kāśī*, Varanasi, 1998, p. 97.

SUPĀRŚVANĀTHA

vārāṇasīe puḍavī supaeṭṭhehiṁ devo ya ।
jeṭhassa sukkavāra sidiṇammitādo visāhāe ॥ — 14/532

Supārśvanātha was born under Viśākha *nakṣatra* on the 12th day of the bright half of Jyeṣṭha month. Pṛthvī was his mother and Supratiṣṭhita was father.

CANDRAPRABHA

candpaho candapure jādo mahaseṇa lācchemaha āhiṁ ।
pussassa kiṇha eyārasie aṇurāha ṇakkhate ॥ — 14/533

Candraprabha took birth on the 11th day of the dark half of Pauṣa month under Anurādhā *nakṣatra*. The name of his mother was Lakṣmaṇā and father Mahāsena.

ŚREYĀṀŚANĀTHA

siṁhapure seṅyaso viṇhu ṇariṁdeṇa veṇudevīe ।
ekkārasie phagguṇa sida pakkhe samaṇabhejādo ॥ — 14/536

Śreyāṁśanātha was born on the 11th day of the dark half of Phālguna month under Śravaṇā *nakṣatra*. Viṣṇu Narendra was his father and Veṇudevī was his mother.

In *Uttara Purāṇa* (57/32-58) and *Triṣaṣṭiśalākāpuruṣa Caritra* (4/1/15-26) also mention has been made about the birth and place of Śreyāṁśanātha. In *Triṣaṣṭiśalākāpuruṣa Caritra* the reason for naming him as Śreyāṁśa has also been given[8] according to which when Śreyāṁśa had entered into the womb the whole nation along with all the royal families had started prospering.

jinasya mātāpitārāvutsavena mahīyasā ।
amidhāṁ śreyasi dine, śreyāṁsa iti cakratuḥ ॥

— *Triṣaṣṭiśalākāpuruṣa Caritra* 4/1/86

8. Ācārya Śrī Hastimal, *Original History of Jaina Dharma*, vol. 1, Jaipur, 1971, p. 94.

PĀRŚVANĀTHA

hayaseṇa vammilāhiṁ jādau hi vārāṇasīe, pāsajiṇo ।
pūsassa bahula ekkārasie rikkhe visāhāe ॥

— *Tiloyapaññati*

Pārśvanātha took birth in Varanasi on the 11th day of the dark half of Pauṣa month under Viśākhā *nakṣatra*. The name of his father was Aśvasena and mother Bommilā (Vāmā).

In all the four birthplaces (Bhadaini, Candrapurī or Candrāvatī, Siṁhpurī or Sarnath and Bhelupur) of the aforesaid four *tīrthaṅkaras*, the temples, of both the Digambara and Śvetāmbara sects, related to these *tīrthaṅkaras* still exist and even the remains of the ancient periods have also been found. The exemplary Jaina images of the Gupta period up to the twentieth century have also been found at Sarnath and Varanasi. Signs of old temples are also found in the excavation of Bhelupur. But at present all the temples are of the nineteenth and the twentieth centuries, wherein remains of the Jaina images of the ancient periods have been preserved.

Images of *tīrthaṅkaras* — Ṛṣabhanātha, Ajitnātha, Supārśvanātha, Candraprabha, Vimalanātha, Śāntinātha, Munisuvrata, Neminātha, Pārśvanātha and Mahāvīra have been found in the Jaina temples of Varanasi.

In the Jaina temples of Varanasi most of the images are of Supārśvanātha, Śreyāṁśanātha and Pārśvanātha. The fact that the number of these *tīrthaṅkaras* images is greater than the images of other *tīrthaṅkaras* is the probable proof that Varanasi had been the place of *kalyāṇakas* of the aforesaid *tīrthaṅkaras*. Apart from Śreyāṁśanātha's temple situated at Sarnath, all the other Jaina temples of Varanasi are dedicated to Supārśvanātha and Pārśvanātha.[9]

9. Kamal Giri, Maruti Nandan Tiwari and Vijay Prakash Sinha, *op. cit.*, p. 98.

If large number of the Buddhist art has been found in Sarnath just because it is importantly linked with Buddha, and in the same way, if the remains of Jaina art have been found at Varanasi, for it being the birthplace of Supārśvanātha and Pārśvanātha, then the remains of Jaina art should also have been found from Sarnath as it is the birthplace of Śreyāmśanātha but such clear signs have not been seen. Dayaram Sahani has mentioned nine Jaina images in the publication of a catalogue of Sarnath Museum; nevertheless the differences found among the materials received from the archaeological excavation, in their publication and between the images kept in Sarnath Museum at present constitute the major problem. Although, some Jaina remains have come into light which are important from the viewpoint of Jaina tradition of Sarnath, these cannot be used as a solid proof for a major conclusion. The search for such possibilities should continue.

Positioning the modern Sarnath in the centre, a survey of nearby areas including Siṁhapurī which is situated at a distance of about 1.5 km from Sarnath, have been conducted. The Gazeteer of Varanasi, Museum Accession Register, Excavation Report, all the images exhibited and preserved in Sarnath Museum and the Jaina images of different museums of Varanasi have been exhaustively studied and surveyed. It is a matter of satisfaction that in this context some such proofs have been received on the basis of which it can be established that the Jaina artistic activities existed in Sarnath probably during the sixth to the seventh centuries. This is significant from the viewpoint of the traditional background of Jaina at Sarnath.

In this series of survey and study, the book of Dayaram Sahani has also been consulted as it is based on the materials received from the Sarnath excavation. Since Sahani himself was involved in the collection, classification, registration and maintenance of the materials received from the excavation and at the same time he also carried the works related to the planning and construction of archaeological museum and the installation of the images in the gallery, he had the total knowledge of the materials received from the excavation. He had catalogued these and gave it a shape of the book, *Catalogue of the Museum of Archaeology and Sarnath* (1914). He has also mentioned some Jaina Images in this book. The images mentioned in this book are as under.[10]

Images of Seated Jaina Tīrthaṅkara [Sr. No. B(G)2]

This image of the size 6.5" × 6.5" of *tīrthaṅkara* combined with umbrella has been portrayed in the posture of meditation. Sahani has not mentioned about the mark *śrīvatsa*. This image of the Medieval period has been found in the excavation of 1904-05 session. This image is not available in museum at present.

Sthānaka Jaina Tīrthaṅkara Image [Sr. No. B(G)1]

The hands and feet (size 9.5" × 8.5") of the image are broken. Perhaps the right hand had been in *varada-mudrā* since the deity has been shown arranging his clothes with his left hand. There is also an umbrella on the forehead. This image too has been found in the excavation of 1904-05 session. This image is also not traceable in museum but the mention of *varada-mudrā* and the arranging of clothes signifies it of being the image of the Buddha. Sahani has mentioned the umbrella, but that was not tri-umbrella.

Forehead

Only three foreheads of stone were found, which are said to be of the *tīrthaṅkaras*. The first forehead [Sr. No. B(G-3)] was 6" × 8.7/4" in size, in the background of which the *pīpala* tree has been engraved. This Medieval period forehead was found in the excavation of 1904-05 session. The second forehead was

10. Dayaram Sahani, *Catalogue of the Museum of Archeology at Sarnath*, 1914, pp. 164, 327-28.

found at the depth of 3 ft below the surface of the Vihāra No.1 during its excavation. The presence of an umbrella of snake-fangs on its forehead indicates its being the image of Pārśvanātha. This forehead belongs to the Medieval period. The third forehead [Sr. No. B(G)6] was also found about 4 ft below the surface of the Vihāra No. 1 the excavation of 1906-07 session.

Image up to Chest [Sr. No. B(G)5]

This image was found near the 21st *stūpa* in the groups of little *stūpa*s at the eastern side of the excavated place during the excavation of 1906-07 session. The drawing of the umbrella of snakes in this image of four inches in size links it with Pārśvanātha or Supārśvanātha. Unfortunately, this image is also not traceable at present.

Sarvatobhadrikā or Jina having four Mouths (Jina Caumukhī) [Sr. No. (G)61]

Four unclothed forms of *tīrthaṅkara*s were standing in *kāyotsarga* around the image of *sarvatobhadrikā*. Traditional marks were also engraved on these forms. The size of this image was 2'-10¼" × 1'-11". On one side of this image there was a shape of Mahāvīra combined with his mark of lion while on the other side there was a shape of Ādinātha combined with his mark of he-ox, on the third side there was a shape of Śāntinātha combined with his mark antelope and on the fourth side shape of Ajitnātha combined with his mark elephant (two shapes) were engraved.

It is notable that during the Gupta period in both the places — Varanasi and Rajagir — the tradition of engraving two shapes in place of one shape of mark of *tīrhaṅkara*s was in vogue. Thus, this image of *sarvatobhadrikā* was certainly a Jaina image about which Sahani has mentioned that it was initially kept in Queens College (at present Sampurnanand Sanskrit University). It seems that it was brought to the Sarnath Museum later on. But unfortunately I could not find this image in the exhibited and preserved collection of Sarnath.

Image of Śreyāṁśnātha [Sr.No.(G)62]

This image was 1'-3¼"×1'-11" in size. It is without a forehead and belongs to the Gupta period. This image has been engraved with a *śrīvatsa* mark and is considered to be in Digambara tradition. Sahani has recognized it as an image of the eleventh *tīrthaṅkara* Śreyāṁśanātha on the basis of the shape of rhinoceros engraved on its back. Sarnath is considered as the birthplace of Śreyāṁśanātha and so it is not a matter of surprise if this image has been made here. Unfortunately, even this image I could not find in the museum at present. From the viewpoint of the development process of the marks in the *tīrthaṅkara*'s images, it can be accepted to belong to the last part of the sixth century or the beginning of the seventh century.

Jaina Tīrthaṅkara [Sr. No. (G)63]

Sahani has described an image of *tīrthaṅkara* size 4'-8½"×2'-11" of the post-Gupta period which has shapes of twin *gandharva*s and a halo on either side. According to Sahani it is impossible to recognize them because of the conch-shell, wheel (*cakra*) and lion engraved on its back, but, perhaps he thought so because in the beginning (1914) there was no sufficient knowledge about the evolution of the *jina* images. Actually, lion is the symbol of lion throne, wheel (*cakra*) of the *dharma cakra* and conch-shell would have been used for cognizance. Thus, this image was probably of Neminātha. It is our misfortune that this image also is not available in the museum for investigation.

From the study of the images mentioned in the catalogue of Dayaram Sahani one fact is clear that Jaina images were present in Sarnath Museum and these images were found at different levels in the Sarnath excavation, which provides archaeological support to the background of Sarnath (birth-place of Śreyāṁśanātha) in the Jaina tradition.

In the nineteenth century and in the beginning of the twentieth century the conception of excavation and museum and the initial state of their maintenance as well as the rules and regulations were unlike in these days. It is for this reason that I could not find any Jaina image that has been mentioned by Sahani in the Archaeological Museum of Sarnath at present. But on the other hand, while studying the images kept in the reserved collection of museum for my personal purpose, I along with Dr. Maruti Nandan Tiwari came across two Jaina images. Of the two images one is of the ninth century. This image is of Vimalanātha and is in *kāyotsarga* pose, combined with his mark of hog. The second image is in the form of a symbolic board on which *śrīvatsa*, *triratna* and *dharma cakra* are exquisitely engraved. Dr. Tiwari had seen another part of the head of *tīrthaṅkara* image during his research in which *tri-chatra* was engraved clearly on the head, which was a clear proof of its being an image of *tīrthaṅkara*. Unfortunately, this image also could not be seen.

Before the creation of the Sarnath museum, all the images received from Sarnath were kept in the collection of Queens College (at present Sampurnanand Sanskrit University). Later on these were brought to the Sarnath Museum. Some images have also been transferred to Bharat Kala Bhavan (Varanasi) and to the State Museum (Lucknow). Under survey, I had studied in detail the Jaina images of Bharat Kala Bhavan and the State Museum (Lucknow). In these images no proof has been received which would prove them to be the image of Jaina received from Sarnath. Thereafter I studied both the exhibited as well as the reserve collections of Sarnath. I had also analysed the reports related to excavation. In addition, I had also scrutinized the accession register of the museum thoroughly. Surprisingly, in all the excavation reports prior to Sarnath I did not find any reference relating to the discovery of the Jaina images. Similarly, there is no mention of Jaina image of Sarnath in the Varanasi Gazeteer also. On the other hand, in the Sarnath Museum's Catalogue of Sahani, there is a clear mention of the images of *sarvatobhadrikā, tīrthaṅkara* and Śreyāṁśanātha. In the detailed inspection of the collection of Sarnath Museum along with Dr. Maruti Nandan Tiwari, we have found clear examples of at least three Jaina images whose period is between the post-Gupta period to the tenth century. All the Jaina images of this period belong to the Digambara tradition. In the aforesaid circumstances, on the one hand the mention of Sarnath as the birthplace of Śreyāṁśanātha in Jaina tradition and on the other hand, the finding of Jaina images in Sarnath during the post-Gupta period, holds importance as it indicates the possibility of getting more Jaina images if a further study, survey, and excavations are undertaken. It is quite possible that in the initial state due to the importance of Sarnath, primarily as the centre of Bauddha art, the reorganization and maintenance of Jaina images was not given importance in Sarnath. The fact is that the scholars had not noticed the Jaina art and images for a long time due to which it could not get the requisite importance. But in the context of modern times, the Jaina tradition and art has been a powerful stream of *śramaṇa* like the Bauddha tradition and art, whose flow is uninterrupted like the Vedic Brāhmaṇa and the Bauddha art.*

It is more appropriate to see the entire area collectively for building images. From this viewpoint it can be said that not only the evidence of the Jaina images have been received from Śreyāṁśanātha's birthplace Sarnath, but also sufficient examples of *tīrthaṅkara*'s images have been found from the different areas of Varanasi, the birthplace of Supārśvanātha and Pārśvanātha, whose period extends from the sixth to the middle of twentieth century. Among these the images of

* Since the presentation of this paper, some Jaina sculptures have been exhibited in a showcase in the Sarnath Museum. — Editors.

Mahāvīra, the image of Neminātha with his mark *yakṣa* and *yakṣī,* the image of Ajitnātha with his cognizance of elephant and the image of Pañcatīrthī are prominent which have been preserved in the Bharat Kala Bhavan, the State Museum, Lucknow and in the local temples. Thus, owing to their relationship with Jaina *tīrthaṅkara*s in the traditional background, the carving of the Jaina images at Sarnath and Varanasi had begun in the Gupta period.

This could be a matter of investigation as to how many images were produced and among them how many images are not available now. All of us know that Varanasi and Sarnath were developed as separate centres of art in the Gupta period.

Besides the examples of the museum, a detailed account of the images of Digambara Jaina temple at Sarnath and Śvetāmbara Jaina temple at Siṁhapurī, situated about 2 km in the south of Sarnath (both committed to Śreyāṁsanātha), is also relevant. Although, among the images kept in both the aforesaid temples of the nineteenth and the twentieth centuries, several such examples of images have been found that were built at other places and later on installed in these temples by the devotees. But these add to the confirmation of the Jaina tradition in Sarnath. So a study of both the temples is necessary. Through a personal survey, a total number of three Jaina images were found in the Sarnath Museum. Among them one is the *triratna* stone strip, the second is the image of Vimalanātha and the third is the head of a broken image of *tīrthaṅkara*.

Stone-plate of Śrīvatsa-Triratna (Sr. No. 380)

The stone-plate about 1.5"×1' in size, was probably made for worship. On the basis of the style of this plate it can be said that it belonged to the last half of the Gupta period. The main feature of this plate is the carving of the generally accepted auspicious marks of Jaina *dharma* which are *śrīvatsa, triratna, cakra* (*dharmacakra*) and the pillar with an emblem. Beginning from the left of the plate to right, the first carving is of the pillar with an emblem, which has been engraved on the plinth having three layers. This emblem pillar could be a symbol of glory, because the manner in which the large *śrīvatsa* is marked on the front and the lotus-buds engraved in its lower crown, it connects it with the context and importance of the worship of *śrīvatsa*. *Śrīvatsa* mark has been engraved in a very interesting and artistic way in the middle portion. And at the end the four *triratna*s have been engraved on all the four sides of the *cakra* representing the four directions. This engraving has been done in such a manner that it appears as if these *triratna*s are supporting the '*wheel of the time*' while safeguarding it from all sides. It should be remembered that the four *triratna*s have also been engraved on all the sides of the *āyāgapaṭṭa*s of Kuṣāṇa period found in Mathurā but they have the shape of *tīrthaṅkara* instead of wheel in the middle.

Vimalanātha (Sr. No. 236)

Made of the buff sandstone of Cunar, in this image Vimalanātha has been presented in the posture of *kāyotsarga*, surrounded by the attendants holding flying whisks. The forehead of this image is broken at present. Vimalanātha's cognizance boar (Varāha) has been engraved on the plinth near the feet of Vimalanātha. *Śrīvatsa* mark has been engraved on the chest of the prime hero. This image can be assigned to the ninth century.

The Top Portion of the Tīrthaṅkara Image (Sr. No. 242)

Sized in .43 × .43 metre this broken image has also been made in the buff sandstone of Cunar. Only the right portion of the halo along with the forehead of this image is safe at present. In this image the amiable-faced prime hero has been endowed with curly hairs. This image of a *tīrthaṅkara* carved with big earlobes, glance upon nose and a halo adorned with lotus, must have been eye-catching in its perfect state. Though this image could not be seen at present Dr. Tiwari had seen it earlier and has placed it in the topmost category of Bauddha image. He is the first to identify it as an image of *tīrthaṅkara* on the basis of the three umbrellas (*tri-chatra*) placed on the top. In this image a figure of a flying celestial being wearing a garland has been delectably depicted against the background of clouds on the left side of the halo. The celestial being has the expression of blissful serenity on its face, which shows honour to the *tīrthaṅkara*. Below the celestial figure a *tīrthaṅkara* has been depicted in the posture of meditation (*dhyāna-mudrā*).

Apart from these three images received during the excavation of Sarnath, the mention of some of the other Jaina images would not be out of place here. These images have been received from the Jaina Digambara temple situated at Sarnath and the Śvetāmbara Jaina temple of Siṁhapurī. These images are made of both stone and metal. Stone images have been engraved in white and black marble whereas the metal images have been made of eight metals (*aṣṭadhātu*).

Śreyāṁśanātha Digambara Jaina Temple, Sarnath

This temple is situated close to (south-east) the world famous Dhameka *stūpa* and is dedicated to *tīrthaṅkara* Śreyāṁśanātha.[11] This temple was built in 1824. The image of Śreyāṁśanātha has been installed on the basic platform of the temple. The stone image in black colour has been engraved in the posture of meditation. The write-up of this image reflects that this image was made by Bhaṭṭāraka Śrī Lalitakīrti Jī in Saṁvat 1881 (AD 1824). Śreyāṁśanātha's mark rhinoceros has also been engraved on the plinth. In this write-up a sentence has been engraved which read as under:

dīkṣā, jñāna, kalyāṇaka kṣetre śrī jina pratiṣṭhākārikā

Śrī Jina is consecrated in the area of initiation, attainment of knowledge.

---

11. E.B. Joshi, *Uttar Pradesh District Gazeteer*, Varanasi, 1965, p. 420.

However, the name of Śreyāṁśanātha does not figure in this inscription. According to Sri Badriprasad Jaina, the priest of a temple, the original image was brought from Pabosa (Kauśāmbī) and was installed here. It means that this image was previously installed at Kauśāmbī. According to the priest another image of this size and form was also brought from Kauśāmbī and was installed in the temple at Bhelupur.

Below the original image of Śreyāṁśanātha, the two other *tīrthaṅkara* images are also installed on the main platform. Both of these images are of Śreyāṁśanātha. The first image is of white marble. This image has also been depicted in the posture of meditation like the original image, but it is smaller in size. The mark of sword has been engraved on the plinth of this image. The second image is made of eight metals (*aṣṭadhātu*) and it has also been depicted in the posture of meditation. Both of these images are the examples of a new sculptural art and have been installed in the first half of the twentieth century. In the shrine of this temple behind altar, a stone slab engraved with sixty small images has been put up. All the figures are in meditation posture. Identification of these figures is not possible due to the lack of mark, *śrīvatsa* or inscription.

On the upper walls of the meeting hall of this temple different beautiful figures and narratives related to the *tīrthaṅkara*'s life have been exquisitely drawn. According to the priest of the temple, this drawing work has been done in Vikram Saṁvat 1957 (AD 1900).

Śvetāmbara Jaina Temple (Siṁhapurī, Sarnath)

This temple is situated at Hīrāmanpur village, about 2 km from Digambara Jaina Temple of Sarnath. This place is famous as Siṁhapurī pilgrimage in Jaina Tradition.[12] The present temple was built by Ācārya Jin Kuśal Candra Sūri in Saṁvat

12. Lalit Chandra Jaina, *op. cit.*, p. 13.

1857 (AD 1800). The stone image of Ācārya Jin Kuśala Candra Jī has been installed on the left side of the entrance gate of the temple. It is believed that the 11th *tīrthaṅkara* Śreyāṁśanātha had attained the four *kalyāṇaka*s (pre-birth state, birth, initiation and wisdom (*kaivalya*)), here. Basically, this temple is dedicated to Śreyāṁśanātha. Even on the main platform of this temple an image of Śreyāṁśanātha has been installed as the main deity. Apart from the original platform there are two other platforms in this temple which are attached to the wall at the back upon which several images of *tīrthaṅkara*s have been consecrated. There are 14 images in the temple altogether, out of which five are made of *aṣṭadhātu* (eight metals) and the other images are made of marble. All the metal images are related to Śvetāmbara sect because *tīrthaṅkara*s are depicted wearing clothes in these images. The stone images are mainly made of white and black marble. Images of Candraprabha, Śreyāṁśanātha, Kunthunātha, Muni Suvrat, Neminātha, Parśvanātha and some other *tīrthaṅkara*s are installed here and among all the images, the maximum five images are of Śreyāṁśanātha. The period of the images received from here is between the first half of the fifteenth century to the twentieth century. Description of these images is as follows:

On the main platform of the temple the image of Śreyāṁśanātha has been installed as the main figure. Apart from it, a total number of five other images has been installed on this platform.

On the main platform the image of the prime figure has been engraved in marble and it is bigger in size in comparison to the other images installed on the platform. This image is in meditation posture with its cognizance of a sword engraved on the plinth and the figures of the nine planets and worshippers have been carved in the background. This image was made in Saṁvat 1912 (AD 1885). Apart from the main figure, the cognizance has also been engraved on the back of the Śreyāṁśanātha's image. These images were made in Saṁvat

1897 (AD 1840), nineteenth century and Saṁvat 2042 (AD 1985) respectively. Only the fourth image (Śreyāṁśanātha) is made in *aṣṭadhātu* (eight metals). In this image Śreyāṁśanātha is seated in meditation while the cognizance of the sword could be seen clearly on the back. Apart from these, the eight attainments and the twenty-four *tīrthaṅkaras*, in the background, have been carved as *Jina Caubīsī.* Out of these *tīrthaṅkaras*, the two *tīrthaṅkaras* engraved on both the sides of the main figure, stand straight in *kāyotsarga* posture while the rest twenty-two *tīrthaṅkaras* are in meditation posture.

On the main platform apart from Śreyāṁśanātha, there are images of Candraprabha and Kunthunātha carved in marble. Both the images are in meditation posture. The period of the carving of both the images is Saṁvat 1897 (AD 1840). The marks of *tīrthaṅkara* Candraprabha and Kunthunātha have been carved distinctly on the back as the moon and the *chāga*.

Behind the original platform and attached to the wall, the two other sub-platforms have also been constructed in the shrine of the temple upon which the images of different *tīrthaṅkaras*, engraved in stone and metal, have been installed. On each of the platform four images have been installed; on the first platform one stone and three *pañcadhātu* (five metals) images of *tīrthaṅkaras* have been installed while on the second there are three stone and one *pañcadhātu* (five metals) images. The images on the first platform could be recognized as that of Śreyāṁśanātha, Muni Suvrat and Pārśvanātha by their marks.

The images of Neminātha, Pārśvanātha and the two other Jaina *tīrthaṅkaras* have been installed on the second platform whose description is as follows :

Images on First Sub-Platform

ŚREYĀṀSANĀTHA

In the *pañcadhātu* image of 8 inches in height, Śreyāṁsanātha with cloth is in the pose of meditation. The mark of a sword is engraved on his back. The images of four other *tīrthaṅkara*s have been engraved in the back-ground of this image, among which two images are in *kāyotsarga* and the other two are in meditation posture. Apart from this, the carving of the eight attendants draw special attention. This image was made in Saṁvat 2041 (AD 1984).

MUNI SUVRATA

In the *pañcadhātu* (five metals) image of Muni Suvrata which is about 7 inches in size, the *tīrthaṅkara* has been depicted in a seated and meditative posture. This image has also been shown in clothes like the earlier images. It means it belongs to Śvetāmbara tradition. The cognizance mark tortoise has been carved clearly on the back. This image is of *caturviṁśati* type as the 24 *tīrthaṅkara*s have been depicted in its background. Along with it, the carving of the eight attendants and the *yakṣa-yakṣī* of main deity draw special attention. Each *yakṣa-yakṣī* has been shown having four arms. According to the inscription this image was made in Saṁvat 1534 (AD 1477).

PĀRŚVANĀTHA

In the image of Pārśvanātha, made of five metals and about 7 inches in size, the *tīrthaṅkara* has been depicted as original deity in meditation pose. This image has also been shown with clothes in the Śvetāmbara tradition. The presence of an umbrella with seven snake-fangs in the image and the rings of snake in the backportion attracts attention. The twenty-four *tīrthaṅkara*s have been depicted in the background of this *caturviṁśati* image. Besides, the *yakṣa-yakṣī* on both sides, that is to say the assisting deities of the main deity, are also notable. The mark as well as the arms of *yakṣa-yakṣī* are not clear. There are eight attendants in the background.

This image has been made in five metals and the *Mūlasaṁgha Nandīsaṁgha* recorded in the inscription which is engraved in its background. Along with it the period of creation, i.e., Saṁvat 1490 (AD 1433) has also been given.

JAINA TĪRTHAṄKARA

This image is in meditation posture like the original image. In absence of the mark, the recognition of *tīrthaṅkara* is not possible. This image is engraved in marble and belongs to the twentieth century.

Images on the Second Sub-Platform

NEMINĀTHA

In the image of Neminātha Jina, made of five metals, the *tīrthaṅkara* has been shown in meditation. This clothed image is in the Śvetāmbara tradition. The size of this image is four inches and Neminātha's mark, the conch-shell, has also been carved on the back of this image. According to the inscription on the back this image was made in Saṁvat 1920 (AD 1863).

PĀRŚVANĀTHA

The 20th century image of Pārśvanātha is carved in marble and shown in meditation posture. The umbrella of seven snake-fangs in the image is notable.

JAINA TĪRTHAṄKARA

On this sub-platform, two images of Jaina *tīrthaṅkara*s deprived of cognizance has been engraved in marble. Both the images belonging to the 20th century are of same size and are seated in meditation posture.

6

Sarnath — Jaina Tradition and Reality

S.M. Jain

VARANASI and Sarnath have almost become one today. But such was not the situation fifty years ago. Sarnath had a distinct entity. It has its own history. There had been constructions, especially of the Buddhists from the Maurya period to the twelfth century. Everything had turned to ruins as a consequence of the attack of Qutbuddīn Aibek in AD 1193. Later in 1824, the Jaina temple, in 1910 the Museum, and in 1931 the Mūla Gandhakuṭī were built. In this article, a discussion on the Jaina temple and the Jaina *dharma* in Sarnath is presented.

Jaina Temple of Sarnath

Sarnath is considered to be the birthplace of the 11th *tīrthaṅkara* Śreyāṁsanātha in Jaina *dharma*. Even a temple of Śreyāṁsanātha is here, in which the main image of Śreyāṁsanātha is in black stone. This was installed on Pabhosā hill in Vikarm Saṁvat 1881 (AD 1824) on Friday, the sixth day of the bright half of the Mārgaśīrṣa month. His other image is in white stone, and was installed at Syadavada school in Benaras in Vikarm Saṁvat 2013 (AD 1956) on the fifth day of the bright half of the Māgha month. The third image of Śreyāṁsanātha Svāmī of metal installed in Bhelupur Digambara Jaina Temple of Varanasi on 25 December 1996. There is a stone strip in Devakulikā at the left side of the platform on the back, which has been mentioned as Nandīśvara Dvīpa (island) in the book *Bhārat ke Digambara Jaina Tīrtha*, part 1, 1974, p. 130. This stone slab is made of Cunar stone and is assigned to the tenth century.

On the same page, it is further recorded that there were three images in this temple among which two were in black stone and the third in white stone, all representing *bhagavān* Pārśvanātha. The author of this book is Paṇḍit Balabhadra Jaina. He toured all the places before the 2500th *Nirvāṇa* festival of *bhagavān* Mahāvīra. Though the actual year of the study of Varanasi is not known, it can be said that this position must have prevailed in AD 1972. The author has also mentioned that both the images in black stone were brought here from the temple of Bhelupur. In support of the aforesaid statement of Paṇḍit Balabhadra, in my book *Digambara Jaina Śrī Pārśvanātha Janma Bhūmi Mandir, Bhelupur, Vārāṇasī*, 1996, Varanasi, p. 3, I have also mentioned that both the images were brought from Bhelupur in the sixth decade of this century. The fact is that only the image of white stone has been brought in 1956. The remaining two images in the black stone have been in existence here for long. The evidences supporting its ancient existence are as under:

1. In *Uttar Pradesh District Gazeteer, Varanasi, Supplementary* published in 1998, mention has been made on page 120 that one Jaina temple of *tīrthaṅkara* Śreyāṁsanātha was established at Sarnath in AD 1824. On page 418, it is mentioned that the Jaina hold Sarnath as Siṁhapurī, the birthplace of their *tīrthaṅkara* Śreyāṁsanātha.
2. Page 69 of *A Guide to Sāranāth,* by B. Majumadar in 1937 and reprinted in 1999, mentions that the Jaina temple of Śrī Śreyāṁsanātha was built in 1824. Sri B. Majumadar was superintendent in the Archaeology Department. I have come to know from the Archaeology office of Sarnath, Varanasi, that he was posted at Sarnath for some time. Thus, he must have seen the image of Śrī Śreyāṁsanātha in 1937.

3. In *Archaeological Survey of India Report*, part I, page 107 Alexander Cunningham has mentioned that he had supervised this area in 1835. The modern Pārśvanātha temple was then situated near Dhameka *stūpa*.

Thus, the image of Pārśvanātha had been in existence since 1835, and it existed till the time of Paṇḍit Balabhadra Jaina. Thus it can be said that the image of Śrī Śreyāṁsanātha was present there before 1937. Where this image of Śrī Pārśvanātha exists at present, is not known. Who built this temple is also not known. The donor of the land and the builder of the temple is believed to be Śrī Chajjūmal. The date of endowment of this temple is also not known. The name of the donor of Śrī Śreyāṁsanātha's black stone image, installed in 1824, is engraved on its footback as "Shri Hiralal" (as per information provided by Shri Prakasha Jaina). This place was uninhabited in 1824 and why he erected this temple is open to guess.

Śvetāmbara Jaina Temple of Hiramanpur

Śvetāmbara Jaina temple is situated at Hiramanpur village, 2 km from Sarnath. It is honoured as the birthplace of Śreyāṁsanātha. In the *Vārāṇasī Jaina Tīrtha Darśana,* written by Lalitchandra Jain of Varanasi, 1997, it is mentioned on page 13 that the temple of Śrī Śreyāṁsanātha of Siṁhapurī was built by Ācārya Jina Kuśalacandra Sūr in Vikram Saṁvat 1857. An inscription depicting this information had been displayed on the entrance gate of the temple which had later vanished during the recent renovation work. I myself have witnessed a stone fixed on the gate of the temple which informed that the renovation work of this temple was done by Ācārya Jina Kuśalacandra Sūri in 1857. This writing is different from the write-up mentioned in the aforesaid book. It is not known whether this inscription is the one which was seen by the writer mentioned above. The correct time of its construction is also not yet known. It is also mentioned in this book that "some years before during the expansion work, some images were brought from the temple situated at Aṅgrejī Koṭhī, Sahu Gvaladas lane and were honourably placed here." Thus, it is unknown which image was placed there at the time of building of the temple and what inscription was written on it.

In Varanasi Janapada along with the birthplace of Śrī Śreyāṁsanātha, the birthplaces of Śrī Candraprabha, Śrī Supārśvanātha and Śrī Pārśvanātha are also in existence. On these three birth-places the Śvetāmbara and Digambara temples exist in equal number. This implies that the followers of the Śvetāmbara and Digambara sects are unanimous about the birthplace of the three *tīrthaṅkaras*. But regarding the birthplace of Śrī Śreyāṁśanātha, they hold differing views — the Digambaras hold Sarnath as his birth-place while the Śvetāmbaras believe Hiramanpur was his birth-place.

Description of Remains in Archaeological Literature

Sir Alexander Cunningham had started archaeological research in 1834 of the three sides of the Digambara Jaina Temple of Sarnath. Digambara Jaina Temple of Sarnath had already been completed before it. Colonel C. Mackenzie had also made some investigation in AD 1815, but there is no record of such investigations.[1] Even before him, Divan Jagat Singh had excavated Caukhaṇḍī *stūpa* in AD 1794 in order to acquire bricks. The work of excavation, according to the rules, started in AD 1834 and continued up to AD 1940. The remains obtained from this excavation have been kept in the Sarnath Museum. But some antiquities are also kept in Kolkata. Most of these remains belong to the Buddhism. Some objects belong to Brahmanism. But were not any Jaina antiquities found here?

An old guide of here informs that the head of an image of Śrī Pārśvanātha was exhibited in Brahmanical gallery. It was removed from the exhibition during the visit of Dr. Shankar

1. Dayaram Sahani, *Catalogue of the Museum of Archaeology at Sarnath*, 1972 (English), Varanasi, Delhi: Indological Book House, p. 111.

Dayal Sharma, the then President of India, to the Museum at Sarnath. Why was it done, it is unknown. Looking at the catalogue it seems that this image is B(G)4. In this catalogue of Sarnath collected by Dayaram Sahani, on page 328 a mention has been made of a Jaina image numbered G-63. About this image it is mentioned that this is exhibited in a big hall at the eastern part of the Museum. Some Jaina exhibits are now on view in the Sarnath Museum.

Five other Jaina images are also mentioned in the catalogue on page 164 whose numbers are B(G)1, B(G)2, B(G)3, B(G)4, B(G)5. Numbers G61 and G62 are mentioned on page 327 and 328. In the description of image No. B(G)1 Cīvar and gift-bestowing posture has been mentioned which is certainly the sign of Bauddha image.

In the aforesaid book namely *Bhārat ke Digambara Jaina Tīrtha*, it is written on a photo numbered as 38, "The ancient *tīrthaṅkara* image of seventh century was found from digging Lucknow Museum." The author Dr. Maruti Nandan Tiwari, in a description of photo no. 18 in *Pratimā Vijñāna* 1981 Varanasi, on p. 293, has mentioned it as one of the images of the Sarnath Museum. Thus we get the record of ten Jaina images and among which the nine images should be at Sarnath Museum and the remaining one at Lucknow Museum.*

Search of Images

The search of the aforesaid ten images was made to start by a young scholar named Dr. Santi Svarup Sinha. For this purpose the direction and blessings of a leading scholar of Jaina images named Dr. Maruti Nandan Prasad had been sought and some financial help was received from Satyendra Jaina, Rajadhani Flour Mill, Delhi.

Nandīśvar Dvīpa Sahasrakūṭa Caityālaya

A stone slab is present in Digambara Jaina temple, which has been mentioned as Nandīśvara Jinālaya by Paṇḍit Balabhadra

Jaina. Some of these types of stone slabs are kept in the museum and the others are kept in the store of the museum. These have been mentioned on page 202 and 203 in the catalogue and number of these slabs are C(B)18 to C(B)25. These are mentioned as part of a *stūpa* similar to *stūpa* D(B)8. All these figures are in meditation posture and Cīvara has not been found anywhere. Sahani has apprehended in the aforesiad catalogue that in the description of C(B)18, these figures could belong to *tīrthaṅkara*. Thus, in this context, there is the possibility that these stone objects could be parts of Jaina Nandīśvara Dvīpa or Sahasrakūṭa Caityālaya.

Stūpa

Sahani has mentioned in the description of the image, number B(G)2 on page 164 of the aforesaid catalogue, that two *stūpas* have been shown on both sides of the umbrella in *tīrthaṅkara*'s image.

7

Jaina Contribution in Early Sculptural Art and Varanasi

R.C. Sharma

THE contribution of Jainas towards Indian culture has been enormous and it is particularly superb in the field of sculptural art. No definite period can be assigned to the beginning of this valuable convention. The nude torso from Harappā is often cited as the representation of *jina* and if it is accepted as such, the sculptural art goes to the hoary past. This solitary, rather controversial piece is certainly an excellent specimen of plastic art. Its perfect curves and contours, fine physiognomy and stiff but expressive posture suggest a high degree of craftsmanship. If this was the case in about 2500 BC one can very well speculate a long background of artistic development even before the creation of this marvellous piece.

The history is silent for a big span of about two millenniums and it is only in the first century BC that a *jina* finds mention in the record of achievements of King Khāravela of Kaliṅga. It further traces back the history of the installation of the deity by about three centuries. We are confronted with obscurity as the image that was originally worshipped in Kaliṅga and taken away to Magadha as a war trophy and again restored to its provenance, now remains lost to the human memory. The Lohānīpur nude torso in the Patna Museum poses the same problem as the Harappan forerunner.

Mathura finally breaks the ice and provides an important and foolproof evidence of the regular commencement of Jaina sculptural art from the second-first century BC. The real contribution is the unbroken sequence of Indian plastic art for the next ten centuries. There was a phase of transition from symbols to anthropomorphic form and it is unmistakably witnessed through the *āyāgapaṭa*s — tablets of homage — belonging to the first century BC. The auspicious motifs which also served as religious and decorative designs present a feast to the eyes. These skilfully and beautifully chiselled renderings are full of rhythm, delicacy and movement. The entwined scrolls and twisting maidens (*dikkumārikā*s) both convey the sense of pulsating life and its vital force.

The grace of nature finally bows to the pious souls and their supermundane penance and austerity. Consequently, a tiny *jina* figure steals the show and gradually it continues to grow to become the focal point. The victory of self-control and attainment of Supreme Knowledge (*kevala jñāna*) which had a solid foundation of non-violence (*ahiṁsā*), is one of the greatest virtues of mankind as it is the life belt for all beings. This maxim is well reflected in the life narration of all *tīrthaṅkara*s and their representation in the sculptural art. Undoubtedly, it was a noble contribution of Jaina community to the society in the realm of art.

The credit of evolution and development of divinities or icons in other religions directly or indirectly goes to Jainism. The Jaina *āyāgapaṭa*s inspired Buddhism to switch over from symbols to image worship. There was no canonical injunction in Jainism to adopt idols while the early Buddhist philosophy did not favour it. This inspiration was the key to success of early sects and was responsible for the widespread of their thoughts. While Jainism preferred to remain confined to India, Buddhism crossed all barriers and earned global reputation within a few centuries.

Jainism is known for its policy of tolerance, mutual understanding and adjustment and this has been well propounded by the theory of Anekāntavāda or Syādvāda, a big contribution to the Indian philosophical thought. The seeds of this benevolent idea were sown in the sculptural art as well. The Jaina iconography at the early and initial stages, particularly at Mathura, did borrow the basic elements of image-worship from the *yakṣa* cult which was in vogue in different forms in the pre-Christian centuries. At the same time the early Jaina icons influenced the plethora of other pantheons to a great extent. Later, in the post-Gupta period, continuing in the medieval age, Jainism assimilated almost all the Brahmanical divinities like Gaṇeśa, Durgā and Mātṛkās.

Learning and dissemination of knowledge has been a marvellous contribution of Jainism. This is evident from the rich libraries of manuscripts and books known as Sarasvatī Bhaṇḍāras which gained footing in the Jaina establishments. *Māthurī Vācanā* in about fourth century AD, aimed at collecting, compiling and analysing the scattered canonical literary traditions. This anxiety and care is already marked through an image of Sarasvatī recovered from Kankali Tila, Mathura. The deity seated in the squatting posture holds a book in the left hand. The Brāhmī epigraph dated to the year 54, corresponding to AD 132 also mentions this image as Sarasvatī *pratimā*. This being the earliest figure of the goddess of learning is itself a remarkable contribution of Jaina iconography. Thus both literary and sculptural traditions corroborate each other at an early stage. The deity appears in the Hindu or Brahmanic art much later and one has to wait for about seven centuries to have a glimpse of Sarasvatī.

Epigraphs and sculptures almost go hand in hand from the very beginning in Mathura Jainology. The Brāhmī inscriptions in beautiful calligraphy on the *āyāgapaṭas* and the images are excellent documents which shed valuable light on the contemporary society and particularly the Jaina culture. The pedestals also furnish the year, month, season and day of installation of the image meticulously. It is rather surprising that the Gāndhāra sculptures carved in the same period and near to the occidental mannerism are devoid of this great merit. These inscriptions are rare, and date is rarer, even if dated the era recorded remains controversial, and one is bewildered to note this confusion. It is rather impossible to frame a convincing chronology of the Gāndhāra sculptures. On the other hand, the Mathura sculptures, both Buddhist and Jaina, help us a lot through their epigraphs in pursuing a scientific study of the development of art and iconography.

The trend initiated in ancient India continued in the later period and a good number of stone and metallic sculptures bear inscription which assist us in identifying the deity, the year of consecration and the donor. The sculptural rendering was marked with improved refinement and delicacy and the stone seems to have transformed into wax at the Dilwara temples where every inch of space breathes and vibrates and one is just wonderstruck to see the grandeur of this great monument. This and several other monuments are the laudable contributions of Jainas in the sculptural and architectural realm.

The notable contribution is that this prosperous community always came forward for upholding and propagation of high and benevolent ideals of peace, co-existence, austerity, penance and sacrifice and also transliterated them in the artistic representation.

Varanasi has been held in high esteem in Jainism, for the traditions bestow on it the honour of the birth land of four *tīrthaṅkaras*, i.e., Supārśvanātha (7th), Candraprabha (8th), Śreyāṁśanātha (11th) and Pārśvanātha (23rd). Of these four, only Pārśvanātha is regarded as a historical person belonging to the ninth-eighth centuries BC. About the earlier three pontiffs the history is silent and we have to depend mostly on the literary texts. Even for Pārśvanātha no direct light is shed but the critical study of all available sources leads us to conclude that the 23rd *jina* was in existence about two and a half centuries before Mahāvīra, the last *jina*. This must also be pointed out that no contemporary archaeological evidence has come forth to corroborate the historicity of any *jina*.

As already explained the symbolic depiction, a hallmark of introducing religious beliefs, was later transformed into anthropological illustration, towards the end of the first century BC. Unfortunately, no such remains have been unearthed from the region of Varanasi. It is only from about the fifth century AD, i.e., the middle of Gupta period that the sculptural evidence is noticed. There must have been a temple in any of the four spots associated with the *jina*s of Kāśī. The process gained momentum from the post-Gupta period when the marks of cognizance were fixed and the list of twenty-four *jina*s was complete. We do have the sculptural representations of Jaina iconography including the *jina*s, their *yakṣa*s, *yakṣiṇī*s (*śāsana-devatā*s), etc. These can be seen in the collection of different institutions like Bharat Kala Bhavan, B.H.U., Sarnath Museum, Sanskrit University Museum, Pārśvanātha Vidyapeetha, Pārśvanātha Temple, Bhelupur, etc.

The State Museum, Lucknow, housed some important Jaina sculptures from Varanasi, particularly excavated from Rajghata (Some of these have been transferred to the Sultanpur and Gorakhpur museums). These are as under:

Jina No. 48.184, size 66 x 26 cm, *fig.* 1

The vertical stele carved in *ultre-relievo* fashion shows a sky clad *tīrthaṅkara* standing straight in *kāyotsarga* posture. The feet are missing and right arm is damaged. Curly hair is arranged in different tiers. The large earlobes touch the shoulders. The conventionalized lotus bud-shaped half open eyes reflect an inward vision. The broadening of lower lip and a horizontal stroke separating the two lips have added blissful serenity to the expression of the face. There is no trace of *śrīvatsa* mark on the chest which was an important feature of the Jaina icons at Mathura.

Apparently, the figure is devoid of halo but the roundish treatment of the upper two corners suggests an effort for providing a halo which surrounded the entire body of the deity. Thus the back slab itself should have served the purpose of halo. This may be pointed out here that some times the complete body of the pontiff is shown inside an oval halo marked with lotus or beaded border. The trend is seen both at Mathura and Sārnāth.

Made in buff sandstone the sculpture can be assigned to the fifth century AD. The corpulence of the body is indicative of its somewhat primitive treatment and a direct impact of Mathura style on the eastern school of Sārnāth of sculpture. The absence of any *yakṣa* and *yakṣiṇī* as attendants suggests that this feature had not yet emerged or did not gain popularity.

Pārśvanātha No. 48.182, size 57.5 x 33.5 cm, *fig.* 2

The sculpture represents the 23rd *tīrthaṅkara* Pārśvanātha in the usual *kāyotsarga* pose. The spiral locks of hair are treated in several tiers taking a conical shape. The enlarged eyes are wide open and the big earlobes suspend on the shoulders. The neck is incised with lines and the same treatment is given on the waist. The *śrīvatsa* mark is noticed in the centre of the chest. The body of the *jina* is slim and straight. A seven-hooded cobra with coils in the background serves as canopy. The incised marking give a realistic rendering of the snake hoods.

A divine musician sitting on the three-tiered cushion above the cobra plays on the drum (*devadundubhi*). The upper side corners are occupied by the two flying celestials with wreaths on either side. The back slab below the celestials is carved with two other *jina*s seated cross-legged on lotus seat in meditation. Thus the sculpture is an example of *tritīrthī* with depiction of three *tīrthaṅkara*s including the main figure of Pārśvanātha in the centre.

The deity is flanked by *yakṣa* Dharaṇendra on the right side. Wearing a snake aurieole round the head, earrings, pearled necklace and other ornaments, he holds a full vase on the left hand while the right hand rests on the knee. His counterpart *yakṣiṇī* Padmāvatī on the other side carries a fly-whisk (*camara*). Her hairs are tastefully arranged and divided horizontally into two parts. Following Dharaṇendra she also has a snake canopy with a conspicuous hood in the centre. Her ornaments are pearled necklace touching the breasts, armlets and wristlets. The lower garment is fastened with a band. Both these flanking figures are slightly bent forming a *tribhaṅga* pose. To the left is seen a devoted kneeling female, with hands clasped in adoration. Traces of lotus petals are noticed below the feet of the main deity on the pedestal which is also carved with *cakra* (wheel of law) flanked by rampant lions.

Made in buff sandstone the sculpture is a superb representation of the post-Gupta period, the seventh-eighth centuries AD. To us this stele with Dharaṇendra and Padmāvatī as attending *yakṣa* and *yakṣiṇī* appears to be one of the earliest representations in the Jaina iconography as the scholars have attributed this type of illustration to the later period. The corpulency has given way to the slender delineation.

Pañcatīrthī 48.183, size 56.5 x 30.5 cm, *fig.* 3

The stele represents five *jina*s seated cross-legged in meditation on separate lotus seats. Each is attended by two *caurī*-bearers or *yakṣa*s and the divine drum beater is also marked on the top of each *jina*. In case of the second *jina* in the upper left corner the scene of the *devadundubhi* is damaged. The stele is divided into two compartments. The *jina*s are seated in two rows and the lower compartment displays *yakṣa* and *yakṣiṇī*s?

The five *jina*s from their cognizances could be identified as Aranātha (fish), Vimalanātha (boar), Śāntinātha (dear), Ṛṣabhanātha (bull), and Pārśvanātha (snake canopy). Ṛṣabhanātha occupies the central place in this Pañcatīrthī. The three *jina*s have the matted hairs arranged upwards and Ādinātha has in addition a cluster and some locks falling on the shoulders. Pārśvanātha on the other hand is shown with curly hairs. The *śrīvatsa* mark is conspicuous on the chest of three *jina*s.

The lower compartment or the pedestal represents male and female figures with children.

The sculpture is made in buff sandstone and should be assigned to the eighth century AD.

Padmaprabha 48.178, size 36 x 32 cm, *fig.* 4

The stele probably represents the 6th *tīrthaṅkara* Padmaprabha (as recognized by the cognizance lotus on the pedestal) in the *kāyotsarga* pose. Hairs are arranged in the spiral lock fashion. The large eyes are three-fourth closed imparting an inward vision. *Śrīvatsa* mark is seen in relief on the chest. There are two meditating *jina*s seated on pedestal projecting from the back slab. The figures of the attending celestials are considerably damaged. In the present context the *yakṣa* should be Kusuma or Puṣpa and *yakṣī* Acyutā or Mānasī. The pedestal shows the cognizance lotus flanked by two rampant lions. One corner of the pedestal is occupied by a mutilated figure of the seated Ambikā holding a child while on the other corner is seen a meditating person whose head and posture of sitting suggest that it is a male figure but the bulging breasts are indicative of female treatment. This iconographic complexity can be interpreted differently. Could it be an illustration of Mallinātha who is sometimes shown as lady in the Śvetāmbara tradition? The upper part of the sculpture is damaged hence the depiction of hovering celestials and the divine drum beater is missing. Made in buff sandstone, the piece should be assigned to the tenth-eleventh centuries AD. It is now in the Sultanpur Musuem.

Jina 48.177, size 29 x 25 cm, *fig.* 5

The slab represent a *tīrthaṅkara* in *kāyotsarga* pose. The hair arranged in tiers of curls and *śrīvatsa* mark is seen in the centre of the chest. There is a plain halo round the head and the top is occupied by the divine drum beater. On either side is seen a hovering celestial carrying a garland. The side jambs of the back slab are carved with four meditated seated *jina*s. Thus, the illustration is of *pañcatīrthī* but the main deity cannot be identified as the lower part of the stele comprising the pedestal and cognizance is broken and missing. Below, are seen two flanking attendants in *tribhaṅga* pose holding fly-whisks.

Made in buff sandstone it should belong to the tenth-eleventh centuries AD. It is now in the Sultanpur Museum.

Tīrthaṅkara 48.179, size 36 x 15 cm, *fig.* 6

Fragmentary sculpture representing a *jina* standing in *kāyotsarga* pose in penance. Traces of curls are seen in the hair and the earlobes are ususally elongated. The damaged halo round the head shows lotus petals and beaded strings. Beneath the right arm of the *jina* is seen the bust of an attending *yakṣa*. Portion below the knee including the pedestal is missing.

Made in buff sandstone the sculpture should be dated in the tenth-eleventh century AD. It is now in the Gorakhpur Museum.

Ajitanātha 49.199, *fig.* 7

Stele representing second *Jina*, Ajitanātha in *kāyotsarga* or *daṇḍa* pose in penance with lock in hair and elougated ears. Half halo issues from the head. A pair of elephants is seen below on the pedestal. The sculpture in puff stone should belong to the seventh century AD.

This fact is also to be taken into consideration that there is always a margin of some confusion between the seventh and 23rd *jina,* i.e., Supārśva and Pārśvanātha, because of the common attributes. Even the association of Supārśva with Varanasi as birth-place may be reviewed on the same presupposition. From the inscriptions discovered from Mathura, it is gathered that Supārśva commanded a high respect even before the Kuṣāṇa period and a *stūpa* put up in his honour was known as *devanirmita,* i.e., built by gods. A large number of statues with a snake-canopy overhead has been recovered and the same may be identified as Supārśva or Pārśva images, unless specified in the epigraph. Similarly, some spots are closely associated with Candraprabha, i.e., the eighth pontiff and a site known as Candrawal is an important citation.

8

Jaina Sculptural Art of Kāśī

M.N.P. Tiwari

JAINISM has been one of the three main religious streams of India which was basically a religion of sramanic (ascetic) tradition. Jainism developed around the 24 *jinas* or the *tīrthāṅkaras* who represent the basic tenets of Jainism, i.e., deep austerity and absolute renunciation. Kāśī has been the place of confluence of all the principal Indian religions namely Brahmanical, Buddhist and Jaina. Its importance in Jaina context is apparent from the tradition, according to which out of 24 *jinas*, four were born in and around Kāśī, and they are Supārśvanātha (7th *jina*), Candraprabha (8th *jina*), Śreyāṁsanātha (11th *jina*) and Pārśvanātha (23rd *jina*). Of these, Pārśvanātha, who is considered to be a historical *jina* and who is usually assigned to the time of eighth century BC, occupies the most venerated position in Kāśī, so far as the images and temples of the *jina* are concerned. As a consequence Kāśī becomes the place of Jaina pilgrimage.

In the ambience of Kāśī we come across plenty of ancient and medieval Jaina vestiges in the form of icons and temples. The most important of such examples are found from Rajghat and several other places in Varanasi (Bhelupur, Bhadaini, Mata Anandamayi Ghat, Ramghata and Maidagin) as well as from Sarnath. The Jaina remains from Kāśī belongs mainly to a period from the sixth century AD to the twentieth century AD. These remains are affiliated to both the Śvetāmbara and

Digambara sects and most of the temples are dedicated to Supārśvanātha and Pārśvanātha. Besides a few images of Ṛsabhanātha (1st *jina*), Vimalanātha (13th *jina*), Neminātha (22nd *jina*) and Mahāvīra (24th *jina* and senior contemporary of Buddha) whose lives are not associated with Kāśī, the images mainly of Pārśvanātha and Supārśvanātha are found in abundance. Surprisingly, the images of the *jina*s like Neminātha and Mahāvīra are prior in date.

Although we do not have any surviving ancient Jaina temple in Kāśī, yet on the basis of the antiquity and continuity of Jainism in Varanasi, as established by the association of the four *jina*s with Kāśī and also on the basis of the reference found in the "Varanasi-kalpa" of *Vividhatīrthakalpa* (of Jinaprabha Sūri of fourteenth century AD) mentioning about the Pārśvanātha temple of Varanasi, it may be postulated that some ancient Jaina temple must have been in Kāśī, which in all probability might have been dedicated to Pārśvanātha. At least up to the tenth-eleventh centuries AD we find only a few *jina* images but they exhibit all the important early stages of the development of *jina* images. These *jina* images are either seated cross-legged in *dhyāna-mudrā* or standing erect in the *kāyotsarga-mudrā* with the *śrīvatsa* mark in the centre of the chest. The usual *aṣṭaprātihārya*s like *siṁhāsana,* fly-whisk bearing attendants, *trichatra, prabhāmaṇḍala, aśoka* tree and divine musicians are also carved with the *jina*s.

One of the earliest images from Varanasi represents Mahāvīra which is now preserved in the Bharat Kala Bhavan, Varanasi (Acc. No. 161). The image datable to sixth century AD, is particularly significant because it is one of the earliest examples which shows the cognizance of the *jina* which in the present case is lion. The graceful image exhibits all the features of the Gupta image which are to be seen in its plasticity, serenity, elegance and animation. The body contours reveal the vegetative rhythm. The image shows a wonderful synthesis between the external form and the inner meaning with the result that the figure reveals the height of spirituality. Mahāvīra absorbed in deep meditation is seated without the *trichatra* on a throne decorated with *viśvapadma* and showing two small figures of lions on two sides of the *dharmacakra* in the centre. The undecorated but graceful halo is specially attractive. The two lions of *siṁhāsana*, meant to support the throne, are carved in *jina* images only at the extremities of the throne. But the extremities of the throne in the present instance are occupied by the diminutive figures of two seated *jina*s and hence the two lion figures of this image stand for the cognizance. It may be noted here that the present image also bears a testimony to the prevalence of the convention of showing the cognizance of the *jina*s in pairs on two sides of the wheel, the earliest instances of which are found at Rajgir (Bihar). This perhaps is the solitary image of Mahāvīra belonging to the Gupta period and showing the cognizance.

Another image of equal importance represents Neminātha which is found from Rajghata and is presently preserved in the Bharat Kala Bhavan, Varanasi (Acc. No. 212; *fig.* 1). The image, datable to the seventh century AD, is one of the earliest images which contains the figures of *yakṣa* and *yakṣī*. Even in the absence of conch cognizance of Neminātha, the image could be identified with Neminātha on account of the figure of his *yakṣī* Ambikā (shown with two babies) and also a palm tree which is associated with Balarāma who was the cousin of Neminātha.

The whole composition in the present image is divided into two parts, being separated in the middle by a stone projection, showing lotus pattern designed below it. In the upper part is carved the seated figure of the *jina* with usual *trichatra*, lion-throne, fly-whisk bearing attendants, and nimbus, while on the lower part are carved the figures of his *yakṣa* and *yakṣī*. This is a clear departure from the tradition wherein the figure of *yakṣa* and *yakṣī* are placed on the right and left extremities of the throne.

fig. 1

The dated images in the *jina* temples of Kāśī on the basis of our survey mainly range in date between AD 983 (Vikram Saṁvat 1040) and AD 1963 (Vikram Saṁvat 2020) (*figs.* 2 and 3). A few images of Neminātha and Vimalanātha respectively with conch and boar cognizances are preserved in the Supārśvanātha Jaina temple at Bhadaini and Sarnath Museum (Acc. No. 236). These images are datable to tenth-eleventh centuries AD. The main Supārśvanātha Jaina temples of Śvetāmbara and Digambara sects are situated on the bank of river Ganges at Bhadaini. These temples were built in AD 1768 and AD 1855 respectively. On the other hand, the Pārśvanātha temples are more in number and they are situated mainly at Bhelupur, Maidāgin, Golghar, Nariya, Khojawa and Ramghat. Of all the temples of Pārśvanātha, the temple at Bhelupur, traditionally accepted as the birth-place of Pārśvanātha, are most important from the viewpoint of their magnificence and the images preserved therein. One very magnificent Śvetāmbara temple of Pārśvanātha has been built at Bhelupur in 2001. This temple is built in western Indian style.

fig. 2

fig. 3

Pārśvanātha Digambara Jaina temple of Bhelupur preserves an important dated image of Ṛṣabhanātha (AD 983). Ṛṣabhanātha with bull cognizance sits in *dhyāna-mudrā* on the lion-throne having the figures of *navagrahas*. The image is important because it shows on the throne not only the figure of Cakreśvarī *yakṣī* (of Ṛṣabhanātha) but also the figures of Ambikā *yakṣī* (of Neminātha) and Gajalakṣmī. The *yakṣa* with lotus and fruit is not bull-faced and hence could not be identified as Gomukha *yakṣa* of Ṛṣabhanātha.

A few *jina* images of tenth-eleventh centuries AD are found from the steps of Lalita Ghat and from the Sitala temple of Prahlada Ghata. These figures deserve immediate attention for their proper preservation and display in some museum. Two figures representing the parents of the *jinas* are also preserved in Śītalā temple of Prahlāda Ghat.

In the Pārśvanātha Jaina temples of Bhelupur, we not only find the images of Pārśvanātha with seven hooded snake canopy but also the independent figures of his *yakṣī* Padmāvatī. In two such figures of Padmāvatī, dated AD 1491 and preserved in Pārśvanātha Digambara Jaina temple, Padmāvatī with three hooded snake canopy and the figure of Pārśvanātha carved over her head is shown in one case with *kukkuṭa vāhana*. In accordance with the texts, the four-armed *yakṣī* holds lotus and goad in two hands while the two other hands show *varada-* or *abhaya-mudrā* and a lotus (or a rosary). In the images of Supārśvanātha and Pārśvanātha the *jinas* are shown respectively with five or seven hooded snake canopy. However, in one example from Pārśvanātha Digambara Jaina temple, Pārśvanātha with snake cognizance is shown with nine hooded snake canopy. The image is dated in Saṁvat 1664 (AD 1607). Besides, the image of Ṛṣabhanātha, Ajitanātha and Munisuvrata could also be noticed in the temple. These images are dated in Saṁvat 1925 (AD 1868).

Thus, it can be concluded that the Jaina art of Kāśī was equally rich in content and style and it still awaits detailed survey and study.

Bibliography

Giri, Kamal, M.N.P. Tiwari and V.P. Singh, *Kāśī ke Mandir aur Mūrtiyān*, chapter 9 on Jaina Mandir aur Mūrtiyān, Varanasi, 1998, pp. 97-103.

Tiwari, M.N.P., *Elements of Jaina Iconography*, Varanasi, 1983, pp. 1-13, 44.

Vividhatīrthakalpa (of Jina Prabha Sūri), ed. Muni Sri Jinavijaya, Singhi Jaina Granthamala 10, Calcutta-Mumbai, 1934; Moti Chandra, *Kāśī kā Itihāsa* (2nd edn.), Varanasi, 1985, pp. 198.

9

Ancient Jaina Culture and Scattered Rare Images of Varanasi

Munni Pushpa Jain

As many as sixteen *janapadas* like Kāśī, Kośala, etc., are mentioned in the ancient Indian literature. Among these Kāśī has always been famous. Earlier, Varanasi city was in the Kāśī *janapada*, but now Varanasi itself is a *janapada*. It is commonly accepted that the name Varanasi was derived from its location between the rivers Varuṇā and Asi (Assī). The famous Jaina poet, Banarasidasa has also mentioned:

> *gaṅgāmāhi āī dhasī dvai nadī varunā asī* ।
> *bīca basī banārasī nagarī bakhānī hai* ॥

> There are two tributaries of the river Gaṅgā called Varuṇā and Asī and between these is situated the city called Varanasi.

The name Benaras is derived from Varanasi, but it is notable that in Prākṛta Jaina Āgamas and other Jaina scriptures, the word "Vanarasi" has been mentioned in place of "Varanasi." The word Vanarasi seems to be more suitable from the viewpoint of the word "Benaras."

Varanasi is situated on the banks of the holy river Gaṅgā. It is the oldest cultural city of the world and renowned in the fields of spiritualism religion, culture, literature, art, etc., and endowed with grandeur. It is the centre of religious harmony, which can be seen evidently in the different religio-cultural traditions, temples, images and remains here. It is a prominent centre of Vaidika and Śramaṇa traditions (Jaina and Bauddha).

Repeated mention in Jaina Āgamas and post-Āgama Jaina literature, besides it being the birthplace of four *tīrthaṅkaras*, are indicative of the fact that Varanasi *janapada* had been a prominent centre of Jaina culture and the same is true in the present days too. But surprisingly, what to speak of common people, even historians were not ready to accept this fact.[1] But after having discovered the images of many *tīrthaṅkaras*, slabs and other remains of archaeological importance in the excavation of Rajghata, the people started to admit the fact that "Varanasi" is a prominent centre of Jaina religion and culture too. In 1990 during the reconstruction of the Digambara Jaina temple at *tīrthaṅkara* Pārśvanātha's birthplace Bhelupur, many small and big ancient images, pillars and other material of archaeological importance, and belonging to the period from second-third century to the ninth century were discovered while digging for the foundation of the temple. Apart from the images, etc., many ancient incidents have also proved the existence of rich Jaina culture here.

Thus, Varanasi has been associated with Jainism since ancient times. Varanasi was one of the kingdoms established by the first *tīrthaṅkara* Ṛṣabhadeva in his area of action. Akampana was its king. It is mentioned in *Jayodaya Mahākāvya* written by the famous poet Bhūrāmal Jī Śāstrī, that the army chief of the early king of India Cakravartī Bharat Mahārāja had presented himself in the *svayaṁvara* of Sulocanā, daughter of the then king of Kāśī and had married her. This incident is said to be belonging to the third era. This was the "early *svayaṁvara*" among the *svayaṁvaras* arranged in India. The great poet Hastimal Ji has also described this in his *Vikrānta Kauravam*,

1. Vijaya Prakash Singh, *Kaśī Ke Mandir*, unpublished research work B.H.U., 1990.

a Sanskrit drama. The same drama is said to be the source for the plot of *Jayodaya Mahākāvya*. Beautiful farming, abundant richness, folk culture of Varanasi and grandeur of the river Gaṅgā are beautifully presented in this book.

Ādi Purāṇa, written by Ācārya Jinasena, also mentions the remarkable glory of Varanasi.[2] The second part, para 43, *śloka* 124-26 of *Ādi Purāṇa* records that there was a city in the kingdom of Kāśī called Varanasi, which was more beautiful than Amarapurī (capital of heaven) for its unlimited palaces and seemed to jeer at the aerial vehicles of Amarapurī. Such creature was not able to take birth in that Varanasi city, who had committed sins in his earlier births. The soul, who took birth in that city, could not be a sinner even by mistake.

Many ancient and historical incidents of Varanasi are narrated in the Āgama and post-Āgama Jaina literature. Many religious narrations of *Jñātādharmakathā* belong to Varanasi. Varanasi is mentioned in *Prajñāpanā-Sūtra, Kalpa-Sūtra, Upāsakadaśāṅga, Uttarādhyayana Cūrṇi, Antakṛta-daśāṅga, Nirayāvalikā, Āvaśyaka-Niryukti*, etc. Among the 63 great personalities in the Cakravartīs, the narration of 12th Brahmadatta finds place in several Jaina scriptures. According to these narrations, he was the resident of Kāśī. In an account it is mentioned that the ninth Cakravartī Padma had made Kāśī the capital of India and provided it political significance.[3]

Varanasi city, the birthplace of *tīrthaṅkara* Pārśvanātha, was also in the territory of Kāśī in those days. During the period of *tīrthaṅkara* Mahāvīra, 18 republics like Kāśī, Kośala, etc., have been found mentioned in the Jaina literature. All of them were followers of Mahāvīra and they had assembled in "Pāvā city" to celebrate the *nirvāṇa* festival of Mahāvīra, just after

2. Ācārya Jinasena, *Ādi Purāṇa, Parva* 43, *Śloka* 124-26.
3. Paṇḍita Balabhadra Jain, *Jaina Dharma Kā Prācīna Itihāsa* (Ancient History of Jaina religion), Delhi, 1974, p. 362.

his attainment of *nirvāṇa*.[4] Jitaśatru, the king of Kāśī in those times, had worshipped *tīrthaṅkara* Mahāvīra in Varanasi. *Tīrthaṅkara* Mahāvīra had also given discourses at *samavasaraṇa* several times in *caita* named Koṣṭhaka, located outside the city. Rich householder named Culnīpitā and an owner of 24 crore coins (*mudrā*) and abundant richness named Surādeva of this city were among the ten prominent *Śramaṇopāsaka*s (disciples) in the times of Mahāvīra. Mahāvīra accepted king Lakṣa as his disciple in Kāma Mahāvana *caitya*.[5] He also initiated Śaṅkha, another king of this city, for taking *dīkṣā*. The princess of Varanasi was his devotee.[6] Varanasi has also been mentioned in *Tiloyapaṇṇatti, Uttara Purāṇa,* Ācārya Padmakīrti's *Pāsaṇāha-Carit,* Vādirāja's and Ācārya Sakalakīrti's *Pārśvanātha Caritra,* and Brahma Nemidatta's *Ārādhanā Kathā Kośa.*

The famous Jaina Ācārya Samantabhadra of the second-third century was cured from the disease called *bhasmaka* in Kāśī. He had composed *Svayaṁbhūstotra* from which as he recited the prayer of the eighth *tīrthaṅkara* Candraprabha, the image of Candraprabha Bhagavān had appeared. For that wonderful incident this place was named Phaṭemahādeva. It is quite possible that[7] the famous temple, namely, Samantabhadreśvara was also built in the name of Svāmī Samantabhadra Ācārya.

Account of Varanasi as Jaina Pilgrimage

Varanasi is the first halting place for every Jaina pilgrim as it is the birthplace of four *tīrthaṅkara*s and is situated on the way to Sammed Śikhara. In ancient days pilgrimages were performed on foot or by bullock-cart. These journeys were

4. *Uvāsagadasāo,* p. 32.
5. *Tīrthaṅkara Mahāvīra aur unkī Ācārya Parmaparā* (*Tīrthaṅkara* Mahāvīra and his Ācārya Tradition), Part 1, p. 276.
6. Dr. Jyoti Prasad Jain, *Uttar Pradesha aur Jaina Dharma,* p. 38.
7. *Ancient History of Jaina Religion,* Part 1, p. 363.

long and hard and performed in large groups of pilgrims. Those groups commenced their journey ceremoniously under the leadership of an able man. Hundreds of *ācāryas*, *upādhyāyas*, *munis*, *āryikās*, *śrāvakas* and *śrāvikās* were included in those groups. After their unobstructed and joyfully accomplished pilgrimages the groups of pilgrims were honoured along with their able leader at their village or city.

The aforesaid pilgrimages had their unique importance. Written scriptures describing such pilgrimages in detail are available, which are in itself historical documents. Several pilgrimages had also been performed in the leadership of great Jaina *ācāryas*, who had written about those pilgrimages. In these narrations of journeys, a vivacious description has been given about the cities, villages, places of pilgrimage, temples, images as well as the social and religious situation of these places which the pilgrims had come across during their long *yātrā*.

The famous scholar Bhanvar Lal Ji Nahata has highlighted Varanasi as a significant Jaina *tīrtha* by mentioning several such pilgrimages in his booklet *Vārāṇasī* : *Jaina Tīrtha* (Publisher Jaina Saṁskṛti Kalā Mandir, p. 25, Kalakar Street, Kolkata 7, Vikram Saṁvat 2502).

Jinaprabha Sūri's Accounts of Varanasi

Ācārya Jinaprabha Sūri had visited many places of pilgrimage in India along with the groups of Jaina pilgrims in the fourteenth century. He had written the book *Vividhatīrthakalpa* in Sanskrit in which he has given a lively presentation of authentic accounts of these pilgrimages. It was published by Asiatic Society, Kolkata. There are 113 *ślokas* in it, in which there is a detailed account of Varanasi and its Jaina temples. Several ancient Jaina narrations belonging to Varanasi are mentioned in this *tīrthakalpa*. At the end Jinaprabha Sūri has mentioned four parts of Varanasi — 1. Deva Varanasi, 2. Rājdhānī Varanasi, 3. Madana Varanasi, 4. Vijaya Varanasi.

Among these Deva Varanasi is that place where the temple of Viśvanātha Jī is embellished. An image of twenty-four *tīrthaṅkaras*, made in a stone strip, was worshipped in this temple in those days. He had mentioned in his *Saṁgrahakalpa* namely *Chaturviṁśati Mahātīrtha* (*vārāṇasyāṁ viśveśvara madhye śrīcandraprabha*). It means that the basic hero was Bhagavān Candraprabha in the aforesaid image of twenty-four *tīrthaṅkaras* made in a stone strip.

Prabhacandra Sūri had composed *Prabhāvaka Caritra* in Vikram Saṁvat 1334, in which the character of Mānatuṅgācārya showed that Mānatuṅga Sūri was the son of Seṭha Dhanapati of Varanasi.

In the description of visits to Varanasi, Śrī Jinaprabha Sūri has made a detailed account of the visits to the birthplaces of *tīrthaṅkaras* — Pārśva, Supārśva and Candraprabha.[8]

Śrī Haṁsasomamaṇi has made mention of Siṁhapura as the birthplace of Śreyāṁśanātha in the accounts of his pilgrimage to Kāśī in Vikram Saṁvat 1565. In Saṁvat 1609 Puṇyasāgara and in Saṁvat 1661 Jayavijaya, Vīravijaya and Jasakīrti have mentioned about the prayer and worship of *pādukā* (wooden slipper) in Siṁhapurī.

The poet Saubhāgyavijaya has written that "Varuṇā" and "Āśā" are the rivers, between these is situated that city. After the ceremonial worship of the land, the birthplace of Bhagavān Supārśva and Pārśvanātha, he went to Candrapurī, the birthplace of Candraprabha. People here called him Candra-mādhava.

In an account of a pilgrimage, made in Saṁvat 1664, Jayavijaya has mentioned two *jinyālayas*, each at the birthplace of Pārśva and Supārśva. He has mentioned that — first of all I prayed at Caumukha Jī, and then worshipped the *pādukās*.

8. *Vārāṇasī Jaina Tīrtha*, Asiatic Society Kolkata, pp. 9-12.

The image of Pārśvanātha is delightful. There are many images in the courtyard of brāhmaṇas and *maṭhas* in the city.[9]

Śrīvijaya called Bhelupur as the birthplace of Pārśvanātha in Saṁvat 1711-12. He also described his visit to Siṁhapurī and Candrāvatī.[10]

The poet Jasakīrti mentioned in Saṁvat 1669 that many Jaina images were present in several post Jaina temples. Description of visits to Kāśī of many Digambara *munis*, scholars and eminent persons are also available. There is a significant description of the Varanasi pilgrimage in an account of such visits over all the country. This description was made by Gyanacanda of jainī Lahore and was published about a century ago.

The description of a large pilgrimage group of Seth Sri Jawahar Lal Ji and Mulacand Ji Soni of Ajmer is even older than 100 years. These descriptions of pilgrimages automatically prove that the Jaina culture had a deep connection with Varanasi from the very beginning.

Varanasi is the birthplace of four *tīrthaṅkaras*. The 7th *tīrthaṅkara* Supārśvanātha took birth at Bhadaini, the eighth *tīrthaṅkara* Candraprabha at Candravati, the 11th *tīrthaṅkara* Śreyāṁśanātha at Sarnath (Siṁhapurī) and the 23rd *tīrthaṅkara* Pārśvanātha took birth at Bhelupur. They also attained here the four of the five *kalyāṇakas* — pre-birth, birth, penance and wisdom.

On this glorious land, various known, unknown and rare remains, images, etc., belonging to Jaina culture still exist in different areas. Only a few persons have noticed them and they remain neglected for being unknown. If these are not upkept in time, these will vanish or be ruined or missed.

---

9. *Ibid*, p. 16.
10. *Ibid*.

Ancient Scattered Jaina Images

In fact, there is a large number of artistic Jaina images all over India. Of these, some images are established in temples, among which some images are famous for their splendour at home and abroad. Apart from these there are such unlimited images of *tīrthaṅkaras* and their *yakṣas-yakṣiṇīs*, which have been found on the banks of rivers, ponds, under the *pīpal* tree, etc., and also in the post-Jaina temples. All of them are very significant from the viewpoint of history and archaeology. A number of broken/unbroken images of Jaina *tīrthaṅkaras* and their *yakṣas-yakṣiṇīs*, etc., can be easily seen as being worshipped in the name of other deities in Hindu temples in Varanasi *janapada*.

As already stated Ācārya Jinaprabha Sūri of the fourteenth century has furnished a detailed account of the place.[11]

In Saṁvat 1669 the poet Jasakīrti Ji had mentioned that apart from Bhelupur — the birthplace of the 23rd *tīrthaṅkara* Pārśvanātha, and Bhadaini — the birthplace of the 7th *tīrthaṅkara* Supārśvanātha, the five images near Viśvanātha temple belonged to Ṛṣabhanātha and Neminātha. He has mentioned in the memoirs of visits that there was an image of Pārśvanātha near Annapūrṇā, and the devotees worshipped several images in Khamaṇavasahī. We worshipped the red-coloured image of Pārśavanātha with sandal-wood powder, stigma of a flower Kesar, flowers, etc. We, after the worship of Candraprabha near Ṛṣabhanātha, and Vardhamāna Caumukha and Supārśvanātha at Bhaddilapur (Bhadaini Ghat) returned to halt. After visiting Siṁhapurī and Candrāvatī the leader of the pilgrimage performed the third *Kaḍaī Sādharmīvatsala*.[12]

Thus, various references are found in the documents of many pilgrimages which prove that the images of Jaina

---

11. *Jaina Temples of Kāśī* (unpublished research work) p. 258 and *Vārāṇasī Jaina Tīrtha*, p. 8.
12. *Vārāṇasī Jaina Tīrtha*, p. 16.

tīrthaṅkaras were established in several Hindu temples. A number of such examples are also present in modern times. Examples of some Jaina images, which can be seen even today, have been discussed under, a study of which can enable us to estimate the extensiveness of Jaina culture in Varanasi.

The river Gaṅgā and its *ghāṭs* are the identity and glory of civilization and culture of Varanasi, which comprises a history in itself. For example, several Jaina images of the tenth century are established near the image of Ṛṣabhanātha in standing posture in the Śītalā temple embellished at Prahlāda Ghat which are worshipped in other names. There is an image of *tīrthaṅkara* on the way to Lalita Ghata, upon the stairs placed against the wall. This broken image is in a standing emotional posture, accompanied by halo, but without a mark. Several scholars like Dr. Maruti Nandan Tiwari, Dr. Kamal Giri, etc., have mentioned about the Jaina images established in temples on these two *ghatas*. Dr. Vijaya Prakash Singh also mentioned about these images along with their pictures in his unpublished research work *Kāśī Ke Mandir* (pages 261-62).[13] These rare Jaina images are as under.

The main image posited in *khaḍgāsana* (standing) and Digambara posture, in Śītalā temple near Rajghat belongs to the first *tīrthaṅkara* Ṛṣabhanātha. Matted hairs suspended on the shoulders are its main and clear identity. On both sides of this image there are two figures carved in meditation and seated posture. On the upper side, shapes of two *gandharvas* (demi-gods of the heaven of Indra) wearing garlands are also carved. These can be assigned to the tenth century. At this very place, near the same image, a pair of Jaina images belonging to almost the same time are also in existence. In one of the images a woman and a man along with a child in

---

13. Dr. Vijaya Singh, *Temples of Kāśī* (An image based study), Motivator, Dr. Martuti Nandan Tiwari, Guide, Dr. Kamal Giri, B.H.U.

their lap have been depicted. In another image the child can be seen only in the lap of the woman. A fruit is depicted in the hand of man. In both the examples woman and man have been depicted in *lalitāsana*. Between them a tree is carved as a divider. Figure of *tīrthaṅkara* is carved above the tree and figures of *gandharva*s wearing garlands are carved on both the upper ends. On the basis of the marks mentioned earlier, these images could be identified as Gomedha Yakṣa and Ambikā Yakṣiṇī. With this description the image of *tīrthaṅkara* could be identified as Neminātha's image (22nd *tīrthaṅkara*). Generally, all images in this Śītalā temple seem to be in Jaina tradition. A deep and independent study is needed for these images.

Attendants carrying fly-whisks are carved on both the sides of the image in standing posture which is fixed on the lower side on the outer wall of Śaṅkara Jī's temple embellished on the left side of the way to Gaṅgā coming from the stairs of Lalita Ghat. Small figures of two *tīrthaṅkara*s are carved in meditation posture on both the sides of the main image. These images are on the verge of destruction because these are fixed in the lower part of the platform on the way. Scholars assigned these images to the first century? Their protection is necessary.

Another image is placed under a *neem* tree in the street behind the Jaina temple of Chedilala Ji, situated in Bhadaini. This image is famous and is worshipped in the name of "Nanghan Vīr Bābā." No one had paid attention to this image. In (naked) Digambara state and in standing posture, about 3.5 ft in height, this image seems to be ancient. The head of some another deity has been fixed in later times on this headless image, which could be seen clearly. Previously, this image had been such placed under the *neem* tree that it faced north. Later on with the intention to hide this image, it had been replaced so that it may face east. Its feet had been covered in the earth and a heavy coat of vermilion (*sindūra*) was painted over it. Any inscription or mark on it would probably be on the hidden parts (beneath the ground). During 1987-88 Dr. Phulchand Jain Premi had shown this image to the famous iconographist Dr. Nilakanth Parushottam Joshi who identified this rare image as *tīrthaṅkara* image. Many scholars had studied Jaina images and temples of Varanasi, but this image remained unknown to them. This is being mentioned for the first time through this paper.

There are two significant images kept in the archaeological museum of Sampurnananda Sanskrit University. One of them is a markless image in a sitting posture having passionless delightful grace. The second broken image is in standing posture. Its height could have been about 5 ft feet and mark of snake still remains on the back-foot of this image. It is lying unsafe in the open, outside the museum.

Some images, received from Rajghat are kept in Bharat Kala Bhavan (Kashi Hindu University, Varanasi). Several other images of *tīrthaṅkaras* are also kept in Bharat Kala Bhavan. Several four-faced images in standing posture belong to the distant past. The image of *tīrthaṅkara* Mahāvīra in sitting posture, belonging to the sixth century, is also very charming and significant.

Jaina Tīrthaṅkara Images from Rajghat

Authorities of the Eastern Indian Railways and Archaeology Department had made excavation at Rajghat, situated on the Gaṅgā banks in the city of Kāśī. Several Jaina images, received in that excavation are kept in the Archaeology Department of the State Museum. These images prove the richness of Jaina dharma during the Gupta period. Images are made in buff sandstone (Cunar stone). Introduction of these images is as under.[14]

---

14. Madan Mohan's "Ramghat se Prapta Jaina Murtiyān," *Candābāī Abhinandan Granth.*

IMAGE OF *TĪRTHAṄKARA* PĀRŚVANĀTHA

Combined with seven fangs, the image of *tīrthaṅkara* Pārśvanātha is in standing posture (*kāyotsarga*). On both the sides two other *tīrthaṅkaras* seated in meditation are carved. On the right side a *yakṣa* holding a vase and on the left side Padmāvatī holding *bījapūraba* are depicted. The upper side is occupied by flying celestials throwing flowers. A tri-umbrella (*trichatra*) is placed on the fang of snake upon which a divine musician playing on the drum is sitting. The plinth of the image is adorned with traces of lotus petals and rampant lions. Above the plinth on the left side near *yakṣī,* a woman is carved in worshipping pose. Probably, this image was gifted by this lady.

SLAB WITH IMAGES OF FIVE TĪRTHAṄKARAS

Images of five *tīrthaṅkaras* along with *yakṣas-yakṣīs* are carved on this stone slab (Register No. 8, 183, size 1' 11 × 1'). The first *tīrthaṅkara* Ādinātha has been depicted in the middle of the second row. Matted hair suspended on the soulders is its particular feature. On the right side of the *tīrthaṅkara*'s image, an image of the 11th *tīrthaṅkara* Śreyāṁsanātha has been carved which is combined with his mark rhinoceros. His birthplace is Siṁhapurī (Sarnath) in Kasi. On the left side of the image of Ādinātha, an image of Pārśvanātha is carved in meditation pose which is combined with the fangs of snake. In the upper row on the right side of the image, an image of the 8th *tīrthaṅkara* Candraprabha, combined with his mark half-moon is carved in the posture of meditation. On the left side of the image is carved an image of the 22nd *tīrthaṅkara,* Neminātha along with his mark — conch-shell (*śaṅkha*). On the lower part of the stone slab, which is similar to the plinth, is carved a *kalpa* tree, under which are *yakṣa-yakṣinī* having a child in their lap, with a mass of praying devotees (human) around them. The upper side is occupied by flying celestials offering flowers.

On this aforesaid stone slab, out of five images of *tīrthaṅkaras* three represent *tīrthaṅkaras* Candraprabha, Śreyāṁsanātha and Pārśvanātha, whose birthplace is Kasi. It seems that the entire illustration has been made for these *tīrthaṅkaras* who belonged to Kasi and the place of origin of these images is also Kasi. All these coincidences are complementary to each other. There is yet another *tīrthaṅkara's* image (size 2.4" × 10") in *kāyotsarga* pose whose mark has vanished. The image is magnificent. Stone slabs representing 24 *tīrthaṅkaras* have also been found. Jaina images are carved in stone slabs as elevated carved images and as *sarvatobhadrikās*.

IMAGE OF AJITANĀTHA IN PILLAR

Image of the second *tīrthaṅkara* Ajitanātha has been carved in the standing posture on a pillar (Register No. 49.54, size 31" × 10"). Figures of two elephants are carved on the base of the plinth, which are shown carrying in full-bloom the double lotus along with its stalks. Since the mark of Ajitanātha is also elephant, the scholars have assigned the period of this image to the seventh century. This image is kept in the State Museum, Lucknow.

Thus, many images have been found from Rajghat. The scholars have accepted this place as a prominent place of Kasi, where remains, belonging to the period about eighth century AD to thirteenth century, have been found on a different levels during the excavation.

Apart from these, in other areas adjacent to Kasi many images have been found. In the temple of the village Manjhava, near Kasi, there are several images of Pārśvanātha and to bring together the other images too, a total number of 32 images have been established at the same place. Several significant remains have been found at Sarnath and Candravati. Certainly, the land of Candravati is filled with a wonderful store of Jaina Culture. An image of the 13th *tīrthaṅkara* Vimalanātha, had also been found in Varanasi. Belonging to the ninth century, this image is carved with his mark boar. This naked (Digambara) image is headless and it is fixed on a simple plinth in the *kāyotsarga* pose. Two attendants on both the sides are carrying fly-whisks.

BIRTHPLACE OF PĀRŚVANĀTHA AND REMAINS FOUND THERE

There are three Jaina temples in a large proximity at Bhelupur, the birthplace of Pārśvanātha, in Varanasi. Of these, two temples belonged to the Digambara tradition and one belonged to the Śvetāmbara tradition. There are also several old and delightful images present in the Śvetāmbara temple and some Digambara images have been placed from the very beginning on the main plinth of this temple. Those images were shifted to the Digambara temple after their amiable division, about 18 years ago. A new splendid temple has been built in AD 1990 at the place of Digambara temple. In this temple several old and new images of different *tīrthaṅkaras* have been installed on its three plinths. Even the Śvetāmbara temple has been splendidly and artistically reconstructed and has been established in AD 2000, which is perhaps one of the worth-seeing places of Varanasi. There is an excellent Digambara Jaina temple embellished on the main road, and was built by Udayarāja Khaḍgasena in AD 1868. Several *tīrthaṅkaras*' images have been fixed on the three plinths in this temple. Along with these images a charming and grand image of Padmāvatī, the *yakṣī* of *tīrthaṅkara* Pārśvanātha, has been placed.

Even if we study the aforesaid two temples from the viewpoint of its ancient origin, we will find that these were not older than three-four hundred years. However, several images which are placed in these temples are earlier than the temples themselves. None the less these images and temples were not considered of specific importance from the viewpoint of archaeology. But during the course of digging for the foundation of new construction at the place of ancient

Digambara Jaina temple, the remains of the ruined temples, older than the present old temple, and the *tīrthaṅkaras'* images of different periods and different types began to appear in three layers. People were wonder struck and had happy feelings because this temple as well as the area belonging to the birthplace of *tīrthaṅkaras* had earlier association. If the whole excavation had been done seriously and patiently then it was quite possible that more earlier specimens would have been found. Two scholars have made a deep study, from the viewpoint of archaeology, of the remains received from the foundation of Bhelupur temple. An article belonging to this study, written by Prof. Sagarmal Jain had been published in the volume of April-June 1990 of the research journal called *Śramaṇa* published from the Parshvanatha Vidyapeetha, Varanasi. The same article has also been published in the research journal *Saṁskṛti Sandhāna* (Part 3, 1990). Sri Satyendra Mohan Jain has also presented his findings in a pictorial booklet, having 14 pages, published in December 1996 (on *pañcakalyāṇa pratiṣṭhā*).[15]

The main images and remains received from this temple are as under.

IMAGE OF PĀRŚVANĀTHA

This broken grand image of the 23rd *tīrthaṅkara* is in the seated (*padmāsana*) posture. It is established on the plinth made by the coil of a grand snake. The same snake, which is endowed with coils, rises in circles and adorns the forehead by its seven fangs. Made in buff sandstone (Cunar) this image of a ruined temple would have been the image of the principal deity. At present the broken image is 39 inches in height and 39 inches in width, but this would have been about 5 ft in height along with neck, forehead and fangs of snake. Scholars assigned it to be of about fifth or sixth century. Half portion of the upper

15. *Booklet of Dr. Satyendra Mohan Jaina*, p. 8.

seven fangs of the forehead of the same image was found during the digging operation of the foundation, which is kept near the same image along with many images for exhibition in the hall below the temple. The forehead portion of an image was also found. In the centre of its brow, on its upper side, an eye-shaped mark *tilaka* has been carved. Some scholars have observed it as the third eye. Some people believe it to be the forehead of the same image. But it does not seem to be tenable.

FOUR-FACED IMAGE IN A PILLAR

Head of a pillar is very significant among the remains found in excavation. Four fine images of different *tīrthaṅkara*s have been carved around it, and belonged to the post-Kuṣāṇa and pre-Gupta period (about fourth century). These images are endowed with passionless, delightful appearance. One of their foreheads is broken, the rest part is safe. Bull, Snake and Lion marks of Ṛṣabha, Pārśva and Māhāvīra respectively are clear and the mark of the fourth image is not carved separately. This image is embellished in beautiful sitting posture (*kamalāsana*). As the mark of the sixth *tīrthaṅkara* Padmaprabha is lotus, so this is identified as his image. All these images are 9 inches in height and 7 inches in width.

Another image up to navel in the sitting posture may be assigned to the fourth century. One bust represents the 16th *tīrthaṅkara* Śāntinātha and it can be assigned to the sixth century AD. It has the mark of an antelope, though not clear, is carved on its back foot. Another good image, 2 ft in height, in standing posture, combined with attendants and illegible inscription, has also been kept in this temple. The left cheek of its face is broken. On the uppermost part and on both sides, two little *jina* images each on the top and the bottom are carved in standing and meditation postures respectively. On both the sides of the feet, a couple is sitting in a praying posture. Probably, this couple represent donors. This image was found in the basement, and not in the digging operation of the foundation. Only one or two words have been deciphered from the inscription of this image. These words are *jayapatiḥ a-r* . . . .

Top portion endowed with unclear write up of a pillar has also been found. Only a few words of its inscription have been deciphered as under — *oṁ* (*mahā*) *rājaśrī bhojadeva mani* . . . *ka* . . . *haṭa śrī kacchama* (*vī*) . . . (*laṁ*) *kāritaṁ*). Dr. Sagarmal says that although there have been many kings in different times in the name of Mahārāja Bhojadeva, but, the person referred to is perhaps the king of Kannauj of the ninth century.[16] Probably he had renovated this temple.

Thus, many remains of images and ancient temples — large bricks, top portions of altars, broad stones for rubbing sandal-wood, remains of pillar, etc., — available here are of much significance. On the upper side of the three platforms many fine Digambara images are incised with inscriptions, which mention *ācāryas*, *bhaṭṭārakas*, cities belonging to the tenth-nineteenth centuries. Many beautiful images of the twentieth century are also present. In the same manner in the Jaina temples embellished at Ramaghata, Sutatola, Bhadaini, etc., and also in the Jaina temples namely Nariya, Khujavan, Panchayati Mandir most of the images belonged to the seventeenth-twentieth centuries.

Thus, Varanasi *janapada* has been the important centre of the rich Jaina culture from the beginning particularly for the fact that it has the pride of being the birthplace of four *tīrthaṅkaras* and the land of visits, *cāturmāsa* (fast of four months) and discourses of other *tīrthaṅkaras*. It has also been the land of spiritual activities and creation of literature.

---

16. Dr. Sagarmal Jaina, *Saṁskṛti Sandhāna*, Part 3, 1990.

10

Kāśī and Banārasīdāsa and Vṛndāvanadāsa

J.L. Jain

KĀŚĪ is a vibrant and eternal place of pilgrimage in India where all the religions — Vedic, Jaina, Bauddha, Islam, etc., have joined hands. Situated on the banks of the holy Gaṅgā this city has been the centre for many cultures and civilizations since ancient times. It is said that no one sleeps hungry in this city of Bābā Viśvanātha (Śiva) and Annapūrṇā (Goddess of food).

According to Jainism Kāśī is the birthplace of four *tīrthaṅkaras* — 7th *tīrthaṅkara* Supārśvanātha, 8th Candraprabha, 11th Śreyāṁśanātha and 23rd Pārśvanātha. The last was the son of the King of Kāśī, either Aśvaśena or Viśvasena of the ninth century BC and it is a historical fact.

Tathāgata Gautama Buddha had also promoted *dharmacakra* (wheel of religion) delivering his first discourse to the five *bhikṣus* (Buddhists) in the forest called Mṛgadāva (Isipattana) near Kasi about 2500 years ago. King Aśoka had built the four-faced lion pillar, Dhamekha *stūpa, vihāra,* etc., at Sarnath in the holy remembrances of Bhagavān Buddha.

Significance of Sarnath from the viewpoint of history had been growing since the Maurya period up to Kuṣāṇa, Gupta and further more until the thirteenth century AD.

The two pilgrims of China, namely Fa-hyana in fifth century and Huen-tsang in the seventh century had visited Kāśī for special study of Bauddha *dharma*. They had come there after bearing lots of difficulties.

Historians considered Kāśī *janapada* or Kāśī city as about 3500 years old. Mahārāja Dhanvantari, the founder (initiator) of *Āyurveda*, etc., was also born at Kāśī. Ādi Śaṅkarācārya, Rāmānuja, Vallabhācārya, etc., had also proclaimed *dharma* here. Sant Kabīra, Gosvāmī Tulasīdāsa, Caitanya Mahāprabhu, Sant Ravidāsa, etc., had also enhanced (promoted) the grandeur of this city. Tulsīdāsa had composed his incomparable book, *Rāmacaritamānasa* in Kāśī and took renunciation of body here. It is just for this reason that there are thousands of temples and places of adoration in almost every lane and every home in Kāśīdhāma.

History and Culture

The Paippalāda section of *Atharvaveda* mentioned that Kāśī was the kingdom of an enemy. An oldest literary reference reveals that Mahāgovinda, the Prime Minister of King Renu, who was the son of Viśvāmitra, had founded Varanasi. Dhṛtarāṣṭra was the first king of that kingdom.

Kāśī was the *janapada* or kingdom and Varanasi was its capital. Later, the words Kāśī and Varanasi came into vogue for one city in common use. Many descriptions have been found regarding the name of Kāśī or Varanasi.

1. King of Kāśi, in the 12th generation of Manu, had founded Kāśī.
2. For the reason of its location between the rivers Varuṇā and Asī (a drain at present) it acquired the name Varanasi. The word "Nāsī" had been found in the place of "Asī" in old scriptures.
3. It has been called the area of the far bank on the Varuṇā river in *Matsya Purāṇa*.

4. According to the *Mahābhāṣya* of Patañjali, this city is situated on the banks of the Gaṅgā.
5. Kapilā (Kapiladhārā) and Vṛṣadhvaja are mentioned in the context of naming of the pilgrimages in *Mahābhārata*.
6. Kāśī has been mentioned in 16 *janapadas* stated in Bauddha and Jaina Āgamas.
7. The country Kāśī is mentioned in *Uttara Purāṇa* of Jaina *ācārya* Guṇabhadra of the ninth century.
8. The famous spiritual Jaina poet Paṇḍita Banārasidāsa of the seventeenth century has mentioned about Kāśī in the first poetic biography of Hindi literature *Ardhakathānaka* :

   gaṅgā māhi āī dhansī dvai nadī varunā asī ।
   bīca basī banārasī nagarī bakhānī hai ॥
   kasināra desa madhya gāṅu tāṅtai kāsī nāuṅ ।
   śrī sudāsa-pāsa kī janama bhūmi mānī hai ॥
   tahāṁ duhū jina siva māraga pragata kīnoṅ ।
   taba setī sivapurī jagata meṅ jānī hai ॥
   aisī vidhi nāma thamai nagarī banārasī ke ।
   aura bhāṅti kahai so to mithyā mata bānī hai ॥

9. Gosvāmī Tulasīdāsa also eulogized the grandeur of Kāśī in the *Vinaypatrikā*. He said that in this *Kaliyuga* the Kāmadhenu (a fabulous cow) like Kāśī should be attended (serving) throughout the life with affection. It is the remover of sorrows, grief, sins and illness and a source of good fortune of all kind. It means that Kāśī has been mentioned as Kāmadhenu.
10. Many archaeological remains, images, utensils, etc., have been found on the Gaṅgā banks towards the east near Kāśī station of Rajaghata.
11. It is believed that the Śiva temple, which is famous as Śāraṅganātha embellished at Saranath was founded by Ādi Śaṅkarācārya.

A scholar has rightly said about it that the vastness of Kāśī lies in the fact that all the devotees of Indian culture coming from the different states seem to bring together their languages, garments and different aspects related to conduct and views. People from different regions such as Bengal, Nepal, Andhra, Tamil Nadu, Maharashtra, Karnataka, Gujarat, Punjab, Kerala, Assam, Utkal, Rajasthan, Tibet, Burma, etc., have dwelled here following their own manners and customs. Followers of Islam and Christianity have also dwelled here. They have also become a part of the culture of this city. Just as the water of the holy Gaṅgā is available for everyone, in the same way the land of Kāśī has always been kind and capable of giving shelter to everyone. Life force has always been fluent here like the current of Gaṅgā water.

The earth or the atmosphere of Kāśī, the holy current of Gaṅgā, the atmosphere of thousands of places of worship (Devālayas), all have such magnetic attraction that whomsoever dwelled at Kāśī once, he did not want to leave it. According to a poet :

> *khāka bhī jisa jamīna kā pārasa hai* ।
> *śahara maśahūra vaha banārasa hai* ॥
>
> It means that the land whose ash is also touchstone that famous city is Benaras.

Of course, Kāśī is a place of rites (*saṁskāra*). In spite of several political, social, natural disasters, floods, etc. Kāśī has been retained and will continue to do so because of its ancient religious and spiritual rites.

Jaina Culture and Kāśī

Just as said earlier Kāśī has been a significant region of Jaina *dharma* and culture too. This land of Kāśī has been the birthplace of four *tīrthaṅkaras*. The four *tīrthaṅkaras* had attained the four *kalyāṇakas* — pre-birth state, birth, penance and wisdom here. It means that it is a prominent pilgrimage place.

The period of the 7th, 8th and 11th *tīrthaṅkaras* is pre-historical and mythological; but the period of the 23rd *tīrthaṅkara* Pārśvanātha is ascertained to be the ninth century BC, which is historical. The place called Kilā-Kohanā would have been the capital of Aśvasena, the father of Pārśvanātha. There is a vast mound there. Recently old images and remains too have been found on the banks of the river in excavation which was done by the Archaeological Department. From the viewpoint of history we can believe that Kāśī has been under the influence of Jaina culture from 3500 years ago.

Bhagavān Mahāvīra took initiation at the age of 30 and attained *kevala jñāna* after 12 years. Later, he performed the spiritual practices and made visits. Although any description of *cāturmāsa* (fast of four months) and also the passages of visits is not available, it can be supposed that like the Buddha he must have visited Kāśī, because Pārśvanātha was his predecessor and Mahāvīra was initatied in his tradition. This incident happened about 2500 years ago. There has been a dialogue between the *śramaṇas* of Pārśva traditions and Mahāvīra traditions. Kāśī has been mentioned in the ancient Prākṛta scriptures of the Śvetāmbara sect like — *Jñātādharma-kathā, Prajñāpanā-Sūtra, Kalpa-Sūtra, Upāsakadaśāṅga, Uttarādhyayana Cūrṇi, Antakṛtadaśāṅga, Niryāvalikā, Āvaśyaka Niryukti.*

In the eighth century scripture *Ādi Purāṇa,* written by Ācārya Jinasena, the incident concerning Satī Sulocanā was related to Kāśī. Ācārya Guṇabhadra, the disciple of Ācārya Jinasena, has also mentioned in his book, *Uttara Purāṇa,* about the birth, etc., of the four *tīrthaṅkaras* among the twenty-three *tīrthaṅkaras* who followed Ṛṣabhadeva. The great philospher, Jaina Ācārya Samantabhadra Mahārāja belonging to the first or second century AD has also illumined Kāśī with his astonishing brilliance and wisdom. It is said that he was suffering from a disease called *bhasmaka*. He performed the duty of a priest in a Śiva temple and he used to satiate himself with the offerings. One day when he was reciting *śloka* in praise of the eighth *tīrthaṅkara*, while composing the *Svayambhū-Stotra*, there appeared the image of Candraprabha. That place exists in Varanasi even today in the name of "Phaṭe Mahādeva." Śivakoṭi was the king of Kāśī in those days.

Jinaprabha Sūri has composed a literary composition in verse called *Vividhatīrtha*. Visits to many Jaina pilgrimages are mentioned in it. He described Varanasi in four parts and also informs that the stone image of 24 *tīrthaṅkaras* was worshipped in the Viśvanātha temple. He has mentioned in his book *Caturviṁśati Mahātīrtha — vārāṇasyāṁ viśveśvara madhye śrīcandraprabhaḥ*. Again, many *ācāryas* have furnished accounts of visits, in which Kāśī has been mentioned as a pilgrimage centre. Many proofs and evidences have been published in this matter. Recently a book has been published with the title, *Bhāratīya Saṁskṛti aur Sāhitya Men Tīrthaṅkara Pārśvanātha* (Tīrthaṅkara Pārśvanātha in Indian Culture and Literature). Ample investigative literary facts have been recounted in it.

The famous talented Jaina poet Paṇḍit Banārasīdāsa has described Kāśı and Pārśvanātha Jinālaya in his autobiography *Ardhakathānaka* composed in the regime of King Akbar. This is the first poetic autobiography in Hindi Literature, which was composed in AD 1641.

This work has religious, social, political, economic and historical significance. Banārasīdāsa has clearly mentioned about the various ups and downs, social situation, political circumstances and mental attitudes of people that he experienced in his fifty-five years of life and these have been inspiring in themselves. Banārasīdāsa has been considered as the founder of *Adhyātma mata* (sect of spiritual matters). Later on this *mata* was established in the Digambara sect in the name of "Terāpantha." Earlier his predecessors were Rājpūts who were initiated by an ācarya in Jaina *dharma* and who bestowed the "Biholiyā" *gotra* (sub-caste) upon the Śrīmāla caste. Jaina ascetic Bhānucandra, a resident of Kharataragaccha was his *guru* (spiritual teacher). Later, he came in contact with *śrāvaka* Arathamalajī of Khairābād. He presented Banārasīdāsa the *Bālabodha Ṭīkā* on *Samayasāra Kalaśa* written by Paṇḍit Rājmalla. While studying this scripture and discussing with his friends he was confused in the context of ritual practices. He gave up all the restrictions and once the four friends even started dancing naked in their room. People used to call them Khosarāmati (confused people). Banārasīdāsa had remained in this state till Saṁvat 1692 (AD 1639). Later, in Saṁvat 1692 he came in contact with Pāṇḍe Rūpacanda. The four friends read the *Gommaṭasāra Grantha,* which revealed to them the balance among the virtues, actions and supreme spirit. Banārasīdāsa then was able to resolve his confusion and he wrote *taba banārasī aure bhayo, syādvāda parinati paranayo.* After that Banārasīdāsa translated *Samayasāra Kalaśa* in Hindi under the name of *Nāṭaka Samayasāra;* which is a significant scripture of doctrine, a spiritual book. The book available these days is the third one. Paṇḍita Nathūrāma Jī Premī has felt that this translation is just independent, original and lively. It is even better than the original *Samayasāra* and *Samayasārakalaśa.*

Apart from the drama *Samayasāra* he composed about 50 books in Hindi poetry like *Nāmamālā, Jina Sahasranāma, Karama Chattīsī, Karma Paddhati Vidhāna, Sūktamuktāvalī.* These works are collected by his friend under the title *Banārasī Vilāsa* in Saṃvat 1700.

It is a matter of surprise that at an early age of 14 he had composed one thousand *dohās* (a rhyming couplet) and *chaupāīs* (quatrains). But when he realized that he had composed such a fabricated story which showed people the path of decline, he had thrown them into the river Gomatī. It is a matter of surprise how he suddenly changed his thoughts?

He was converted into a spiritualist from a totalitarian. He was neither a Digambara nor a Śvetāmbara. He did not entangle himself in such type of secular differences. He has written about his name in the *maṅgalācaraṇa* (pronouncing of a blessing) of the drama *Samayasāra* :

jinhakī janama purī nāma ke prabhāva hama ।
āpano svarūpa lakhyau mānusī jhalaka meṅ ॥

Both the followers of Śvetāmbara and Digambara sects have contradicted spiritualism or Terāpaṅtha of Banārasīdāsa. But he remained fixed to his thoughts and today we see that Terāpaṅtha has spread all over the country. Many shrines have been built belonging to the Terāpaṅtha Āmnāya.

This great poet has mentioned spiritual implications of many illustrations, systems and beliefs, etc., in the drama *Samayasāra.* The spiritual meaning of the seven passions, fourteen jewels (precious stones), names of Goddess Durgā, inherent notion of the nine tastes of literature, etc., given by him are significant. Likewise, he considered mankind to be united. He considered Hindus and Muslims similar. He mentioned four kinds of men from the viewpoint of natural tendencies and nature —

1. Similar to grape (*drākṣā*) or raisin (*kiśamiśa*) — soft inside and outside.
2. Similar to coconut — soft inside, hard outside.
3. Similar to jujube (*bera*) — soft outside, hard inside.
4. Similar to betelnut — hard inside as well as outside.

Banārasīdāsa had married thrice in his life. He got nine children, but all of them had expired. He wrote about it :

nau bālaka hue mue rahe nārī nara hvai ।
jyoṅ taruvara patajhāra dvai, rahe ṭhūṅṭha se hoya ॥

Even tolerating such griefs his poetry vibrated with life. A common man cannot remark in this way. He had seen the death of his maternal grandmother, the birth of daughter and arrival of daughter-in-law on the same day. One can imagine the firmness of his mind in such a situation. Such a great poet was Banārasīdāsajī. He did not dwell in Benaras, but Pārśvanātha and Kāśī had always impressed him.

The great poet Vṛndāvanadāsa Jī was also a resident of Kāśī. The name of his father was Dharaṅgacanda. With his poetry he spread Jaina *dharma* all over India. The *Caubīsī,* the adorations, composed by him have been recited in every Jina temple situated in each village and city. Adorations of 24 *tīrthaṅkaras* have been composed by many other poets too, but the impression of Vṛndāvana's adorations is unique. These adorations filled a devotee with emotion from the viewpoint of word, taste (*rasa*), art of rhetoric (*alaṅkāra*), *rāga*, notion (*bhāva*), and rhythm. The devotees sing these and even sway in the divine pleasure. He composed the book *Chandaśataka* just in 18 days for teaching metres (*chanda*) to his son. He had described not only the notes of the metres but also the meaning of their names. The scenes of Jitendra, Samvasaraṇa, Prātihārya, Atiśaya, etc., have become omniscient at every step in these *padas* (verse compositions) or *kavittas* (Hindi syllabic metres). At the last, in this book, he has mentioned his genealogy too in a unique way.

He has also rendered in verse the expositions of Bhagavad Kundakundācārya, which is rare in these days. The verse compositions (*padas*) and praises composed by him are also famous. He composed *Chanda Śataka* in Saṁvat 1898. The poet who immersed the whole society in the rich taste (*rasa*) of devotion with his poetry, his memory should be made permanent and it is the responsibility of the Digambara Jaina society of Kāśī. A huge amount has been lavishly spent on different functions and shows of the society and hence a memorial should be gratefully built in the memory of one whose name is recited everyday since more than 150 years.

Several organizations in Jaina society are working in the field of education at present. Pārśvanātha Vidyāpīṭha and Gaṇeśavarṇī Jinasena Research Institute are famous for research works. This paper will be incomplete without mentioning Śri Jinendra Varṇī Ji. He stayed here for about fifteen years. It was his effort that *Samaṇasuttaṇi* was composed according to the desire of Vinobā Jī. This is a great achievement from the viewpoint of Jaina society.

I also hold the opinion that the name Sarnath has been developed from Śreyāṁśanātha's another name "Śreyanātha" which later became Sarnath, perhaps owing to its easy pronunciation. Moreover, Sarnath's relations with Isipattana and Sāraṅganātha seem to hold no esteem.

The people of Varanasi are rich, educated, well-mannered and hard working. We do hope that Jaina culture will progress continuously.

Although when thought deeply, a question certainly comes to our mind as to what use is praising history, culture and richness of the past? Cities and civilizations are evolved, developed and ruined in the current of time. Does the counting of richness, splendour and numbers in anyway help in the human development? If we cast a glance on the current of the last 3500 years and make an evaluation of the present, then we will come to know how much the behaviour of man has been affected with this tradition? For this very reason I think we will have to forget the past and learn to live in the present. Impression of *dharma* can be effective in not being just a scholar of *dharma* but in being religious (having to do with *dharma*).

11

Nature and Character of Kāśī

S.K. Sadhak

KĀŚĪ is the oldest city of India. This land was dense with Kuśa (a sacred grass used in Brahmanical ceremonies), was inhabited by the people of post stone-period who made this land the abode of Goddess river Gaṅgā: *devo devī nadī gaṅgāmiṣṭamanaṁ śubhā gatiḥ*. Kāśī has been called Varanasi and Benaras. Even being lower, it is higher than the heaven in prestige. Though bounded to the limits of the world, it gives salvation.[1] When the common people believed in gaining passion and wealth as the aim of life, Kāśī had then searched the philosophy of deliverance from the pleasures and griefs. For this reason those people liked Kāśī who remained harmonious in griefs and pleasures. Kāśī is not only the famous city of the world but it is also the city of Viśveśvara (the owner of the world, Śiva). The current of savour flows here uninterrupted: *yeṣāṁ kvāpi gatiḥ nāsti teṣāṁ vārāṇasī gatiḥ*. It means who do not attain salvation anywhere attain it in Varanasi.[2]

---

1. *bhūmiṣṭhāpī na yā'tra bhūstridivaṭo'pyuccairadhaḥ sthapi vā* ।
yā baddhā bhuvi muktidā syuramṛtam yasyāṁ mṛtā jantavaḥ ॥
yā nityaṁ trijagatpavitrataṭinī-tīre suraiḥ sevyate ।
sā kāṣī tripurāri-rājnagarī pāyādpāyāt jagat ॥
— *Kāṣī Khanḍa*, 1.1

2. *Kāśī Khaṇḍa*.

Significance of Varanasi city[3] has been seen throughout the Indian literature. Varanasi is first among those ten prominent cities which are mentioned in the Jaina scriptures. These cities are — 1. Varanasi, 2. Campā, 3. Mathurā, 4. Śrāvastī, 5. Sāketa, 6. Kāmpilya, 7. Kauśāmbī, 8. Mithilā, 9. Rājagṛha, 10. Hastināpura. It has been placed in the middle among the seven cities in the Sanātana scriptures. 1. Ayodhyā, 2. Mathurā, 3. Māyā, 4. Kāśī, 5. Kāñcī, 6. Avantikā, 7. Dvārakā. Varanasi is placed last among the six names found in the Bauddha scriptures: 1. Campā, 2. Rājagṛha, 3. Śrāvastī, 4. Sāketa, 5. Kauśāmbī, 6. Varanasi. We can suppose that those who have revered the soul and character of Kāśī, have also encouraged the people of Kāśī for objective thinking and relative working.

When Bābā Viśvanātha arrived at Kāśī from Mandarācala the people of Kāśī began anointing him with the cow-milk at Kapiladhārā. It means the people of Kāśī had learnt agriculture, animal husbandry and hospitality before his arrival. This learning began from Ayodhyā. In the pre-historical period Ṛṣabhadeva had founded the principle of *karma* (period of hard working) and spread the Indian culture by educating the people to earn livelihood by the six arts — *asī* (art of fighting with arms), *masī* (art of learning Śāstras), agriculture (art of production), architecture, commerce and literature.[4]

Ṛṣabha delivered the throne of Ayodhyā to Bharat. According to the *rāṣṭrakavi* (national poet) Dinakara "This country is named Bhāratavarṣa in the name of Ṛṣabha's son Bharat."[5] According to an Indian legend about six thousand years ago in the middle of north India, Manu and his descendants had appeared. Manu was the first king of this

3. *Kāśī Khaṇḍa.*
4. *Bhagavān Mahāvīra Smṛti*, part 6, p. 3, Dr. Jyoti Prasad Jain.
5. *Saṁskṛti ke Cāra Adhyāya* (Four Chapters of Culture), p. 129.

country.[6] Ikṣvāku, the eldest son of Manu ascended the throne of Ayodhyā. In Jaina literature, Ajitanātha (Ayodhyā), Sambhavanātha (Śrāvastī), Abhinandana, Sumati (Ayodhyā), Padmaprabhu (Kauśāmbī) and Supārśva and Candraprabha (Varanasi) are the ones who were benefited by the learning of Ṛṣabha, and who adorned the *karmayuga* with grandeur and opened the new horizons of development and developed civilization.

In the 33rd genealogy of Ikṣvāku, the King Hariścandra had donated his realm to *maharṣi* Viśvāmitra in a dream. Early in the morning Viśvāmitra asked for *dakṣiṇā* after having taken the crown, royal dress, ornaments, etc. Then Hariścandra having nothing to give as *dakṣiṇā* got ready to be sold along with his wife Tārā and son Rohita. It was then that the people of Kāśī mustered their courage to pay their price and not to be frightened with the *maharṣi*'s anger. One of those who paid for them was from the higher caste and another one from the lower caste. The residents brought upon the king of Ayodhyā then when the area of Kāśī was not under the sovereignty of Aryans. In *Manu-Smṛti,* composed in the third century BC, it is the middle region which is mentioned as a centre of Vedic civilization and not Kaśī.[7]

Indus civilization was present in the Metal, Bronze and Stone ages. Some scholars considered them as the post-Āryan and southern civilization. According to Pandit Jawaharlal Nehru the oldest tribe of India whose knowhow is known to us is Draviṇa. It had its own language. It had transacted trade with other castes.[8] "Aryans had to fight with *asuras* in the north-west India four thousand years ago." Dravida flighted (escaped) to south and the asuras dwelled in Iran, Sumeriya,

6. Dr. Rajabali Pandeya, *Frācīna Bhārata* (Ancient India), pp. 47-48.
7. Varanasi Gazetteer, p. 25 (1965).
8. *Pitā ke patra putrī ke nāma* (Father's Letters to Daughter), p. 49.

Asiriya and different regions of Western Asia.[9] The young ones of their 15th-16th generation had come back to fight against the Indian rulers which has been called *Devāsura Saṅgrāma* (battle between *deva*s and *asura*s). According to Sir John Marshal the Indus civilization was in vogue during 3250 BC to 1500 BC.

In those period Jaina *tīrthaṅkaras*, namely, Savidhinātha (Kākandī), Śītalanātha (Bhaddilpur), Śreyāṁśanātha (Siṁhapurī/Sārnāth), Vāsupūjya (Campāpurī), Vimalanātha, Anantanātha (Ayodhyā), Dharmanātha (Ratnāpurī), Śāntinātha, Kunthunātha, Amaranātha (Hastināpura), Mallinātha (Mithilā) and Munisuvrata (Rājagṛha) existed, but they were ignored by the historians because of their devotion to non-violence. The unavoidable violence is mentioned in Jaina literature in the life contexts of 12 Cakravartī, 9 Balabhadra, 9 Vāsudeva and 9 Prativāsudeva, among which several contexts are related to Kāśī, which are helpful to link the sequence of pre-Vedic period to the history of *Rāmāyaṇa* period. Instead of mentioning the heroics along with the tradition of Mahāvīra, the latter has been ignored against the encomium of heroics which downgrade his benevolence. Which is more significant — benevolence or ruling? If rulers have been placed first and benevolents the second then the truth, simplicity, forbearance and addition could not be preferred.

The five kings of Ayodhyā, from Ikṣvāku to Rāma, have been mentioned in the *Raghuvaṁśa* of great Kālidāsa. Likewise, the genealogy of Ayodhyā has also been mentioned in Purāṇas. "The composing of texts of Vedas had started from its 18th or 19th generation which had come down up to the 68th generation (King Sudāsa) and even after it for two or three generations. Meanwhile Bharata, the son of Duṣyanta and Śakuntalā and king of Paurava kingdom situated in the northern parts of Doābā (region between the Gaṅgā and

9. Dr. Rajabali Pandeya, *Prācīna Bhārata* (Ancient India), pp. 37-38.

Yamunā), had conquered Ayodhyā and annexed it in his kingdom.[10] He performed Digvijaya (Conquest of the world) and dociled the kingdoms, contemporary to him." Thus after many generations Bhāratavarṣa, which was named in the name of Ṛṣabha's son Bharata, had become Bhārata of Bharata, son of Śakuntalā. Born in similar lineage Hasti established Hastināpura. Later on Bhīṣma, the son of Hastināpura's king Śāntanu, came to Kāśī and kidnapped the three princess — Ambā, Ambikā and Ambālikā for his brothers which became the cause for the great war of Mahābhārata. Later, discontented Ambā became Śikhaṇḍī and caused to lay Bhīṣma on the bed of arrows. The king of Kāśī was killed in that war along with 283 kins and 53,12,840 soldiers (army of 18 *akṣauhiṇīs*). Scholars like Pargiter, Sitanatha Pradhan, Ray Chaudhari have stated that there were 45 generations in *Satyayuga* from Svāyaṁbhuva Manu to Vaivasvata Manu. Like it, 14 generations from Manu to Rāma have been considered to exist in *Tretāyuga* and 39 generations from Rāma to Yudhiṣṭhara in *Dvāparayuga*. "Period of the war of Mahābhārata has been considered to be 1277 BC."[11] During these periods *Maharṣi* Vedavyāsa, the composer of *Mahābhārata* had made the last collection, and had done the edition and classification of Vedas and explained the gist of Purāṇas, about which *tīrthaṅkara* Nami, born in Mathura, also seems to agree.

> *aṣṭādaśapurāṇesu vyāsasya vacanadvayam* ।
> *paropakāraḥ puṇyāya, pāpāya parapīḍanam* ॥

Just after the *Mahābhārata*, in front of the eyes of Śrīkṛṣṇa, the family members of Yadu fought and killed each other. Gambling ruined the family of Kurū and wine ruined the family of Yadu which resulted in the suffering of the whole country. King Ariṣṭanemi, born in Śaurīpura, while going to Junagadha

---

10. Dr. Rajabali Pandeya, *Prācīna Bhārata* (Ancient India), pp. 57-58.
11. Javahir Lal Jain, *Bhārtīyā Śravaṇa Saṁskṛti*, p. 8.

to marry the daughter of Ugrasena, heard with compassion the lament of the animals who were going to be slaughtered for the marriage feast. Listening that he returned from the arched gateway and had started a campaign for providing help to the war afflicted Indian, wiping out the tears of widows, supporting the old mothers and fathers and to take care of the orphaned children. He visited from Dvārakā to Kāśī and Kāśī to Dvārakā on foot that resulted in the purification of thoughts, conduct and food. Millions of Indians had given up flesh eating, gambling and drinking. Methods for giving up selfishness and to be good to others and the attainments of highest truth with this had come into light. "Heaven after death and realm after victory"[12] had been unappetising. Govardhanadhārī Giridhara Gopāla Kr̥ṣṇa had made Braja prosperous and powerful. Keeping it in view the assistants of Ariṣṭanemi had developed many areas like Braja between Girnāra (Gujarat) and Gommaṭeśvara (Karnataka) that have been famous.

It was intolerable for those nature-loving brāhmaṇas who perceived gods as Supreme and the protector of the universe or its particular part, owing to their supernatural powers obtained through their imaginative power. They used to beg abundances like food, son, strength from the gods and prayed for protection from the misfortune and victories over enemies.[13] The practice of *yajña*s like Naramedha, Gomedha, Ajāmedha, Aśvamedha (*yajña*s in which man, cow, goat, horse respectively were sacrificed) performed under their priesthood was coming to cessation and the influence of the *yoga* against *yajña* became more powerful. Profound meditation of Śiva greatly contributed in that influence. Abandoned from Kāśī the *yājñika*s (priests officiating at sacrifices) reached Prajāpati Dakṣa, father-in-law of Śiva, living in the footland of Himālayas for

---

12. *Hato vā prāpsyasi svarga jitvā vā bhokṣyase mahīm* — *Gītā* 2/17.
13. Dr. Nalini Mohan Sanyal, *Purāṇa Sāhitya kī utpatti*.

performing *yajña*. Satī reached behind them without any invitation and told about the epoch-making character of Śiva. When *yājñika* ignored it and blazed up *yajña* with his *mantra*, then Satī too blazed up the fire of *yoga* and sacrificed herself in it: *asa kahi joga agani tanu jārā*. Despite this *yājñika* did not stop *yajña*. Then youths of Kāśī reached under the leadership of Vīrabhadra and destroyed the *yajña* — *jajña vidhvaṁsa jāi tinha kīnhā*. The destroyer of *yajña* was called demon, noctural and monster in *Rāmāyaṇa* periods, but the circumstances changed such that Vīrabhadra, etc., had to be assumed as *gaṇa*s (attendants) of Śiva. (Because satī had sacrificed herself there, at her maternal home Himālaya: *Satī jo tajī daccha makhadevā jananī jāi himālaya gehā*. Later on the same Satī became worthy of reverence for the people of Kāśī as Pārvatī.

The evaluation of the contribution of Kāśī in this sequence of development of culture is yet to be done. Acharya Vinoba while referring to the time-related ritual practices has written:

> At first there were dense forests. Deforestation and burning woods were *yajña* in those periods. Disciples used to bring fire wood from jungles and burn them. When jungles were cut down and the inhabitants settled down then it was assumed that every person should plant a tree like Babūl, Nīm, Pīpal, etc. It was assumed *yajña* in those periods. There was too much cotton in our country, but still clothes were imported. Hence the production of cloth by spinning thread then began to be considered as *yajña*. At the present time production of foodgrains, hard work and the imparting of that yield to society is *yajña*.[14]

As the remarks of Vinoba are not readily accepted by the ritual practitioners, in the same way the new values were not accepted by the *tāpas* like Karmaṭha. It is then that Pārśva, the prince of Kāśī, had blowed the conch-shell of social revolution based on *dharma* in 877 BC.

---

14. *Vinoba Sāhitya*, part 1, pp. 129-43.

Brāhmaṇas, who had abandoned inactivity; kṣatriyas, who had given up arms; vaiśyas who had given up the violent trade and śūdras, who had accepted the services as *dharma*, became his followers. Keeping in mind the utterance *samānaśīlavyasaneṣu sakhyam* (equality of conduct), Ācārya Ratnaprabha Sūri and Svayaṁprabha Sūri had laid four rules for bringing similarity in their ways of life, food and drink, and conduct:

1. Hardworking daily for conversion of passion into action (*karma*).
2. Abandoning of gambling, wine, flesh eating, frequenting prostitutes, adultery, hunting and robbery.
3. Donation, virtuous nature, penance and sharing for the development of society.
4. Having notion of adoration towards the *pañca parmeṣṭhi* of *arihant, siddha, ācārya, upādhyāya, muni*.

Those who adopted these rules have been called *mahājanas*. Thoughts and character of *mahājanas* had been so much refined that *ṛṣis* belonging to the Upaniṣad period had assumed it worth to be followed.[15] *Mahājanas* were the hero of *karma* as well as the hero of *dharma*. They wanted profit but along with the auspiciousness. They loved prosperity but attainment too. Whenever there was an opportunity to prove their valour they applied their entire might. The *dharma* based on social revolution of Pārśvanātha glorified Kāśī.

Kāśī was the kingdom and Varanasi its capital. In those periods the 18 Republics of Kāśī-Kośala, the *dharma* of Mahāvīra (569 BC) was in high repute. Mahātmā Buddha (563 BC) had performed *dharmacakra* (wheel of *dharma*) at Sārnāth. "Kāśī was a prominent centre for trade in those periods. The river Gaṅgā

---

15. *tarkopratiṣṭhaḥ śrutayo vibhinnāḥ naiko muniryasya vacaḥ pramāṇam* ı
dharmasya tattvaṁ nihitaṁ guhāyāṁ mahājano yena gataḥ sa panthāḥ ıı
— *Vidura Nīti*

was the main passage for trade. A trader named Mitra Bindaka had travelled through sea by ship. There was an abundant business of elephants' tusks (ivory) and horses of Uttarāpatha in this city. The region of Kāśī has been famous for cotton farming.[16] The women looked after farms. The whole Bauddha literature is filled with the mention of clothes of Kāśī." Surādeva, Culanīpitā and Mahāśataka of sixth century BC are mentioned in the Jaina literature. Surādeva had 24 crore golden coins (*mudrās*) and Culanīpitā and Mahāśataka had 32 crore golden coins each. One-fourth of this money was invested on farms and home, the second one-fourth was invested on business, the third was kept for dealing with the needy persons and the remaining one-fourth was spent on the service of society. Sukhadeva had 60 thousand cows and Culanīpitā and Mahāśataka had 80 thousand cows each. There was abundance of cow-milk. Hundred pairs of oxen cultivated the farms. Those yields benefitted the people of the country and this resulted in the multi-dimensional development of Kāśī. Digging of wells and ponds was done, *ghāṭas* and temples were built and *dharmaśālās* (rest house for pilgrims and travellers) were established. Arrangements were made in schools for teaching literature, music, and skills of art, grammar, astrology and theology.[17]

The remains found in the excavation of Rajghata have shown that this work was done in those days when the Vaidika society was extended to the far banks of Assī in the south, Varuṇā in the north and Gaṅgā in the east. A *yajña* was performed by Samudragupta at Prayāga in the fourth century AD. Vaidikas earned the rights to dwell in Kāśī as a sort of *dakṣiṇā* (fee paid to a brāhmaṇa for the performance of sacrifice) for that *yajña*. Later, the mingling of the traditions of Āryas-Anāryas, local and foreign, formed the present Benaras. Also

---

16. Dr. Avadhesh Narayan Singh, *Pāṭal*, part 2, p. 8.
17. *Upāsaka Daśāṅga.*

in the last years of the twentieth century, the *mahājanas* of Benaras saved more than 60 thousand cows and oxen which were going on the way to the slaughter house. They started farming that was free from the poisonous chemical fertilizers and pesticides. They made the hundreds of acres of wasteland fertile by using the cowdung and cow urine; opened up cow milk booths; desilted a dozen of Gaṅgā *ghāṭas*, and devoted their physical, mental and material resources for public well-being. An evaluation of these works and a comparative study with other societies should be done so as know who has been benefitted by the glorification of Kāśī and who has adhered to the inner-outer purification and dedication to hard work and peace: *antaḥ śuddhi bahiḥ śuddhīḥ śramaḥ śāntī samarpaṇam.* Chinese pilgrims, Arab scholars and other foreign historians have been impressed with its diversity since 1600 years but at the same time have also indicated their disappointment on seeing its ugliness. Why is it so ? All of us should answer it and make an evaluation of the progress and retardation and also understand the difference between words and actions. In fact, Benaras is not a story of the past. It is a history in itself. It is easy to see this city, but difficult to recognize.

It is a vast land of adoration of *tantra* (incantations), *mantra* and literature. With the change of culture, the voices of *ajānas* coming from the mosques and the ringing of bells from the temples, echoing in all the ten directions, can be heard. The tall towers of Churches along with the domes of Gurudwaras can be seen here. Here the evening and the night appear wonderful when the whole city like the glittering flame of lamps, sleeps such as if it has been covered with the light green garnet of the Gaṅgā along with its delightful grace and wake up like *subahe* Benaras.[18] If the people of Benaras do not ignore the past and establish a balance between the needs of present and expectations of the future, then all the trees could

18. Kamal Gupta, *Sāhityakāra Jo Itihāsa ban gaye, Śivāñjali,* pp. 67-70.

be *kalpavṛkṣa*, all the rivers Gaṅgā, all the tendencies *puṇyapradā*, all the languages Hindi, and the whole of the earth could be Varanasi.[19] Because the consciousness, which makes every *kaṅkara* (pebble) the Śaṅkara (Śiva) and the assuming of *sukṛti saṁbhutana vimala vibhūti* makes the man the Brahmā.[20] With the co-ordination of non-violence, restraint, creativity and meditation man can be the god of gods (Devādhideva). On the basis of the conception of: *aja anavadya akāma abhogī* (unborn, blameless, passionless, indifferent to the pleasure of the senses) Mahādeva, there is a philosophy of Kāśī, which considered the earth better than heaven and assumed Kāśī as unique in the three worlds (*trilokas*) and the men worthy of honour for gods-goddesses.[21]

Since about thousands of years the historians are keen to know the history of Kāśī from the post-Stone Age to the atom-period, but the cultural horizon of Kāśī is extended to 60 thousand years and further up to the *manvantaras* also.[22] The life style of Kāśī, which enables the people to abandon the evils, to obtain the knowledge that should be gained and adopt the worthy deeds, will remain relevant and will be followed in the predetermined world as it is a combination of truth, auspiciousness and beauty: *satyaṁ śivaṁ sundaram*.

sacala acala meṅ antaryāmī bhinna piṇḍa brahmāṇḍa nahīṅ hai ।
kāśī svayaṁ prakāsī nagarī svarga yahīṅ apavarga yahīṅ hai ॥

---

19. *sampūrṇa jagadevanandanavanaṁ sarve'pi kalpadrumāḥ* ।
gaṅgāvāri samastavārinivahāḥ puṇyā samastāḥ kriyā ॥
vacaḥ Prākṛta-saṁskṛta-śrutiṣirau vārāṇasī medinī ।
sarvāvasthitirasya vastuviṣayā dṛṣte parabrahmaṇī ॥

20. *guhya brahma tadidaṁ bravīmi na mānvāt śreṣṭhataraṁ hi kiñcit* ।
— *Mahābhārata*, Śānti 229/20

21. *devāvi taṁ namaṁ santi jassa damme sayā mano* ।
—*Daśavaikālikaḥ* 1.1

22. *avidyayā mṛtyuṁ tīrtvā vidyayā 'mṛtamaśnute* । — *Īśāvāsyopaniṣad*

12

Kāśī, Yaśovijaya and Jaina Institutes

K.K. Jain

FROM several evidences it is known that Paṇḍit Yaśovijaya of Gujarat had visited Kāśī in the seventeenth century. In this context Pandit Gopinatha Kaviraja mentioned that the famous Jaina scholar Yaśovijaya Gaṇi (AD 1608-88) visited Kāśī in AD 1626 for studying *Navya-Nyāya-Śāstra* from the famous Naiyāyika Raghudeva Nyāyālaṅkāra of Kāśī. Paṇḍit Yaśovijaya was 18 years old at that time. It is also famous that he had studied in Kāśī for 12 years (1626-38) in the disguise of a brāhmaṇa. The name Raghudeva is also mentioned in the *Aṣṭasāhasrī*, composed by Paṇḍit Yaśovijaya.

In his childhood Paṇḍit Yaśovijaya was called Jasavanta. He was born in the village Kanodu near Kalol in Gujarat. Name of his father was Śrī Nārāyaṇa and mother Śrīmatī Sobhāgade. Along with his older brother Śrī Padma Singh Ji, he took initiation from Śrī Vijaya Ji Mahārāja at Pātaṇa (Gujarat) in Vikarm Saṁvat 1688.

After initiation Jasavanta was named as Yaśovijaya and Padma Singh as Padma Vijaya. In Saṁvat 1600 Yaśovijaya Ji had performed eight *Avadāna*s in the presence of Saṁgha. Impressed by him a famous businessman there, namely Dhanajī Sūrā, requested Guru Nayavijayajī to prepare another Hemacandra by teaching Paṇḍit Yaśovijaya in Kāśī. For this cause the said businessman had given acceptance to spend two thousand dinar of silver and also remitted money by a bill of exchange. Afterwards Guru Vijayajī came to Kāśī along with his disciple Yaśovijaya where he had learnt Law, etc., for three years from Raghudeva Bhattacharya. It is notable here that according to Pandit Gopinatha Kaviraja, Yaśovijaya had studied in Kaśī for 12 years, whereas Paṇḍit Sukhalāla Jī Saṅghavī held it for three years. What is reality, it is difficult to say, but generally the period of his study in Kāśī is accepted as 12 years. This period seems to be appropriate for a complete study. In addition to it, he was honoured with the title, "Nyāya Viśārada" (well versed in law) for his victory in *śāstrārtha* (a doctrinal debate) with some ascetics.

There also prevailed a rumour that he was honoured with the title, Nyāyācārya. For the authenticity of these incidents, the period of 12 years of Yaśovijaya's stay in Kāśī seems to be correct.

After Kāśī he stayed at Agra for four years where he accomplished a special study and practice of Nyāyaśāstra. Later he went to Ahmedabad and performed eighteen *Avadānas* in the presence of the Sūbedāra of Gujarat appointed by Aurangzeb. Impressed by it everyone assumed him worthy for the degree of Upādhyāya and thus Paṇḍit Yaśovijaya was honoured with the degree of Vācaka Upādhyāya in Saṁvat 1718 by Vijaya Prabhu Suri, the disciple of Vijayadeva Sūri. He was deceased at village Dabhoi near Baroda (Gujarat) in Vikarm Saṁvat 1743.

Upādhyāya Śrī Yaśovijayajī was a scholar of Sanskrit, Prākṛta, Gujarati, Hindi, etc. He was an expert in grammar, literature, law, doctrine, metre (*chanda*) and art of rhetoric. For this reason he had composed many scriptures on various subjects of learning; he did not remain confined to any particular language. He had composed his scriptures in Sanskrit, Prākṛta, Gujarati as well as Hindi. This not only confirms his variegated genius but also his liberal outlook about the languages.

Śrī Yaśovijayajī has also proved his genius by writing books in the original manner on the dull and incomprehensive subject like Navya-Nyāya.

About 70 scriptures composed by Mahopādhyāya Yaśovijayajī Mahārāja have been known yet, out of which nine scriptures are incomplete. He had made a vow to compose 108 scriptures marked with *rahasya pada.* It is unknown, however, how many scriptures could he compose in his life but there are five scriptures that are known namely — *Prabhā Rahasya, Syādvāda Rahasya, Bhāṣā Rahasya, Nayā Rahasya* and *Upadeśa Rahasya.*

The scriptures composed by Yaśovijayajī can be divided into three parts — in the first category comes those scriptures which are available, in the second category comes the incomplete scriptures, and, in the third category those scriptures can be included whose authorship is known from different sources.

Available Scriptures

1. *Adhyātmamata Parīkṣā (Svopajña Ṭīkā),*
2. *Adhyātmasāraḥ,*
3. *Adhyātmopaniṣad,*
4. *Anekānta Vyavasthā,*
5. *Ādhyātmika-matadalanam (Svopajña Ṭīkā),*
6. *Ārādhaka-Virādhaka Caturbhaṅgī (Svopajña Ṭīkā),*
7. *Aṣṭasāhasrīvivaraṇam,*
8. *Upadeśa-rahasyam (Svopajña Ṭīkā),*
9. *Aindrastuti Caturviṁśatikā (Svopajña Ṭīkā),*
10. *Karmaprakṛti Ṭīkā,*
11. *Gurutattva Viniścayaḥ,*
12. *Jñānabinduḥ,*
13. *Jñānasāraḥ,*

14. *Jainatarkabhāṣā*,
15. *Devadharmaparīkṣā*,
16. *Dvātriṁśad Dvātriṁśikā* (*Svopajña Ṭīkā*),
17. *Dharmaparīkṣā* (*Svopajña Ṭīkā*),
18. *Dharma Saṁgrahaṭippaṇam*,
19. *Nayapradīpaḥ* (*Svopajña Ṭīkā*),
20. *Nayopadeśaḥ* (*Svopjñanayāmṛtataraṅgiṇī Ṭīkā*),
21. *Nayarahasyaṁ*,
22. *Niśābhakta-prakaraṇam*,
23. *Nyāya-Khaṇḍa Khādyam-Vīrastavaḥ* (*Svopajña Ṭīkā*),
24. *Nyāyālokaḥ*,
25. *Paramātmapañcaviṁśaṭīkā*,
26. *Paramajyotipañcaviṁśaṭīkā*,
27. *Pātañjalayogadaraśna-vivaraṇam*,
28. *Pratimā Śatakam* (*Svopajña Ṭīkā*),
29. *Bhāṣā Rahasyam* (*Svopajña Ṭīkā*),
30. *Mārgapariśuddhiḥ*,
31. *Yatilakṣaṇasamuccayaḥ*,
32. *Yogaviṁśikā Ṭīkā*,
33. *Vairāgyakalpalatā*,
34. *Yogadīpikā* (*Ṣoḍaśakavṛttiḥ*),
35. *Sāmācāri Prakaraṇam* (*Svopajña Ṭīkā*),
36. *Syādvādakalpalatā* (*Śāstravārtā Samuccaya Ṭīkā*),
37. *Stotrāvaliḥ*,
38. *Saṁkheśvarapārśvanāthastotram*,
39. *Saṭīkā Pārśvanātha-stotram*,
40. *Ādijina-stavanam*, *Vijayaprabhasūrisvādhyāyaḥ*, *Gauḍī-Pārśvanāthastotrādiḥ*, *Dravya-paryāyayuktiḥ*, etc.

Incomplete Scriptures

1. *Aspr̥śad Gativādaḥ,*
2. *Utpādavyayadhrauvyasiddhi Ṭīkā,*
3. *Karmaprakr̥tiḥ Laghuvr̥ttiḥ,*
4. *Kūpadrṣṭāntaviśadīkaraṇam,*
5. *Jñānārṇavaḥ Saṭīkaḥ,*
6. *Tiṅantānvayoktiḥ,*
7. *Tattvārtha Ṭīkā.*

Scriptures not obtained

1. *Adhyātmopadeśaḥ,*
2. *Alaṁkāracūḍāmaṇi Ṭīkā,*
3. *Anekāntapraveśaḥ,*
4. *Ātmakhyāti,*
5. *Ākaragranthāḥ (?),*
6. *Kāvyaprakāśa Ṭīkā,*
7. *Jñānasārāvacūrṇiḥ,*
8. *Chandaścūḍāmaṇiḥ,*
9. *Tattvāloka Svopajña Vivaraṇam,*
10. *Trisūtryālokaḥ,*
11. *Dravyāloka Svopajña-vivarṇam,*
12. *Nyāyabinduḥ,*
13. *Pramāṇarahasyam,*
14. *Maṅgalavādaḥ,*
15. *Latādvyam,*
16. *Vādamālā,*
17. *Jñānārṇavaḥ,*
18. *Vādarahasyaṁ,*
19. *Vidhivādaḥ,*

20. *Vedāntanirṇayaḥ,*
21. *Śaṭhaprakaraṇam,*
22. *Siddhāntatarka-pariṣkāraḥ,*
23. *Siddhāntamañjarī Ṭīkā,*
24. *Syādvādarahsyam* and
25. *Syādvāda-mañjūṣā* (*Syādvādamañjarī Ṭīkā*).

From the viewpoint of the genre some of the aforesaid compositions of Upādhyāya Yaśovijaya are contradicting (revoking), some are expounding and some integrating. Although Upādhyāyaśrī was a Śvetāmbara ascetic, his vision was broad because he had earned knowledge in Kāśī. For this reason whatever he had written, has been written after deep thinking. Previous Jaina jurists have incorporated only the evidences and prudence (Naya) in Jurisprudence, but Yaśovijayajī had given a new direction to the Jaina Jurisprudence by including the deposer (*nikṣepa*) in logic (*tarkaśāstra*), which is his original contribution.

By composing the various kinds of literature, the multifarious brilliant, venerable Upādhyāyaśrī Yaśovijayajī Mahārāja has made such a great contribution in the spread of Jaina *dharma* and philosophy that it can never be forgotten or overlooked. Keeping in view his splendid contribution, the grateful Jainas expressed their gratitude by establish-ing his image at his *samādhi* (place of cremation) at Dabhoi (Darbhāvatī city) in AD 1953. To present reverential offerings to him, apart from the creation of the images, Sri Yaso Bharati Prakasan Samiti, Badodara has published *Śrī Yaśovijaya Smṛti Grantha* in AD 1957.

Earlier in AD 1902 Acharya Vijayadharma Suri Ji Maharaja had founded Śrī Yaśovijaya School in his memory, which has produced Jaina scholars like Prajnachaksu (blind) Padmasri Pandit Sukhalala Ji Sanghavi, a teacher of Jaina philosophy in

Banaras Hindu University, and Pandit Becharadas Ji Josi, the famous and distinctive scholar of Jaina Āgamas.

Besides, *Yaśovijaya Granthamālā* (Series of Scriptures) was also started, in which several useful and original texts have been published.

Presenting my reverential offerings to the honourable Yaśovijayajī Mahārāja I would like to say these words —

nyāye gautama eva ko'pi kaṇabhug vaiśeṣike darśane ।
śabde pāṇinireva yaḥ sambhavat mīmāṁsake jaiminiḥ ॥
syādvāde ca yadīyabuddhiramalā naisargikī taṁ guruṁ ।
nyāyācārya-yaśo-yatimunimahopādhyāya-pādaṁ namaḥ ॥

Apart from the aforesaid two institutions in the name of Mahopādhyāya Yaśovijayajī, there were many other institutions in Kāśī that existed earlier and also many institutions that are still working here, whose brief introduction is as under.

Sri Syadvad College

In AD 1905 Honourable Ganesha Prasad Ji Varni Maharaja had founded Sri Syadvad College as a reaction of the grief he had experienced after the insult from the Jainism. Among the top-notch hundred scholars present in the Digambara Jaina society in the present century, about 90 per cent scholars have studied in this college. The founder of this college has himself been a student of this college. Other notable scholars are as under — Nyāyācārya Paṇḍit Mahendra Kumar Jaina, Siddhāntācārya Paṇḍit Phūlchand Śāstrī, Siddhāntācārya Paṇḍit Kailāscandra Śāstrī, Nyāyācārya Dr. Darbārīlāl Koṭhiyā, Sāhityācārya Paṇḍit Amṛtalāl Śāstrī, Sarvadarśanācārya Prof. Udaya Chandra Jain, Sāhityācārya Prof. Khuśāla Goravālā, Prof. Gokul Chandra Jain, Dr. Komal Chandra Jain and Prof. Sudarshanlal Jain. All these scholars have made Kāśī their working place, so their names have been mentioned here. Apart from these scholars there are more than one hundred scholars who have gained name and fame at home and abroad for their contribution in the fields of literature and social service. Among these scholars Ācārya Jñānasāgarajī Mahārāja, the *guru* of Ācārya Vidyāsāgarjī Mahārāja, who had studied in the same college is notable. The four *bhaṭṭāraka*s of the Jaina Bhaṭṭāraka Pīṭhas, situated in different parts of the country, had also received education at the same college.

There is an old library, namely, Akalanka Sarasvati Bhavan, at Syadvad College, where 15,000 books have been collected. In this collection there are several rare and old scriptures too. A hand-written journal namely *Syādvād* has also been published from here, whose 25 volumes are present in this library even today. "Syādvād Pracāriṇī Sabhā" is an organization of this college which makes the students skilled in art of speech.

There is also a hostel endowed with all facilities of food, etc., for students. This college is gradually getting strayed from its old character.

Parsvanath Vidyapitha

This Vidyāpīṭha was founded in AD 1938 with the collective efforts of Paṇḍit Sukhalalaji Sanghavi, Dr. Vasudevasaran Agrawala, Paṇḍit Dalsukhabhai Malavaniya, etc. About 80 scholars have completed their research work and gained the degree of Ph.D. by taking advantage of this Vidyāpīṭha and about more than hundred foreign scholars have also completed their research work by using the library, etc., of this Vidyāpīṭha. The Satavadhani Ratnachandra Library, situated here, is enriched with Jaina literature. This Vidyāpīṭha has published about 130 significant scriptures and 50-60 booklets. *Jaina Sāhitya kā Vṛhad Itihāsa* (Extensive History of Jaina Literature) and its supplement *Hindi Jaina Sāhitya Kā Itihāsa* (History of Jaina literature in Hindi) have been written and published under the supervision of the same Vidyāpīṭha.

The journal *Śramaṇa* has been published uninterrupted from here since November 1949. Earlier this journal was published monthly, but now it is published tri-monthly. In the beginning there was abundance of social articles in this journal, but now mainly the research works are being published. It also houses a small museum which is being run under the supervision of Sri Surendra Mohan Jain.

Hostel, residence for the workers, guest-house, etc., are provided in this Vidyāpīṭha. Being situated in the fragrant atmosphere it is also considered as a Jaina *āśrama*.

Sri Ganesh Varni Digambara Jaina Sansthan

The disciples of Śrī Gaṇeśa Prasād Jī Varṇi had founded "Sri Ganesh Varni Granthamala" in AD 1947, but after the establishment of Sri Ganesh Varni Digambara Jaina Institution in 1969 the former Granthamālā was merged in it. About 40 scriptures have been published from this Institution till now and some research work has also been done through it. *Jaina Sāhitya Kā Itihāsa* (History of Jaina Literature), written in the viewpoint of Digambaras had been prepared and published in three parts by the very same institute. There is also a small library here. Since the last four-five years, a Siddhāntācārya Pandit Phulachandra Shastri lecture-series is also being organized.

Bhāratīya Jñānapīṭha

Bhāratīya Jñānapīṭha was founded in Kāśī by Sahu Shantiprasad Jain and his scholar wife Srimati Ramarani Jain in order to spread the Jaina literature. This Jñānapīṭha has enabled the editing and translation of many rare scriptures, and prepared many original texts, and has published them. In the beginning this organization was upkept by Prof. Mahendra Kumar Nyāyācārya. A few years ago its Golden Jubilee festival was celebrated. The Jñānapīṭha reward awarded by this organization in the field of literature is well known. This organization is working in Delhi at present.

Vir Seva Mandir Trust

This Trust has published about 60 scriptures till now, out of which 35 scriptures have been published from Kaśī. Dr. Darabarilal Kothiya has been the editor and controller of this series of scriptures. This trust has been transferred to Jaipur now.

Prakrit Text Society

This society was founded in Delhi with the incitement of Muniśrī Puṇya Vijayajī and with the efforts of Rāṣṭraratna Dr. Rajendra Prasad Ji. Its able secretary Professor Dalasukh Bhai Malavaniya was a lecturer of Jaina philosophy at Banaras Hindu University. Thus, it was operated with the co-operation of the famous scholars like Dr. Vasudevasharan Agrawala and Professor Bhola Shankar Vyas. Several original texts of Prākṛta language have been edited and published through this society.

Jaina Sanskriti Sanshodhak Mandal

This organization was founded with the efforts of Dr. Bulacand Ji Jain in AD 1944. It had published 32 small research booklets in AD 1949. Several other booklets have also been published after it. With the help of scholarship granted by this organization Professor Nathmal Ṭāṭiyā had gained the title of D. Litt. from Kolkata University.

Sanmati Jaina Niketan

Outside the premises of Banaras Hindu University and situated at the northern boundary at Nariyā, the "Sanmati Jaina Niketan" was founded with the collective effort of Dr. Mahendra Jain, Paṇḍit Phūlcand Śāstrī, Paṇḍit Pannālāl Caudharī and Paṇḍit Kailāścandra Śāstrī. It has been running a "Jaina lodge" since many years, but its situation is deteriorating from the last 20 years and some people have illegally seized it.

Sri Jinendra Varni Shodh Sansthan

Jainas in the name of Kṣullaka Jinendra Varṇī Jī, have founded this institute, but its progress is slow. The management of

Jinendra Varni Granthamala is also under it. The grateful Jainas society of Kāśī has established an image of Kṣullaka Jinendra Varṇī at Sarnath.

Ashoka Vidya Mandir

This unit was founded by Paṇḍit Amritlal Shastri. It has published two-three booklets uptil now.

Publication of Samaṇasuttaṁ

Accepted by the four sects of Jaina *dharma* the scripture *Samaṇasuttaṁ* was published by the Sarvaseva Sangh, Rajghata, Varanasi. With the incitement of honourable Vinoba Ji, Kṣullaka Jinendra Varni had initially composed the *Jiṇadhammaṁ* then the *Jaina Dharmasāra* and ultimately the finished form *Samaṇasuttaṁ*. Sri Sarad Kumar Ji Sadhak, Krsnaraja Mehta and Jamanalala Jain Sarnath have made a great contribution in the completion of this scripture.

Composing of Jainendra Siddhānta Kośa

Being called the great collection of Jaina principles *Jainendra Siddhānta Kośa* was prepared by the honourable Kṣullaka Jinendra Varni in Kāśī after a deep devotion of 18 years. This task was performed at Chedilala Jain temple in Bhadaini. This scripture has been published in five volumes by Bhartiya Jnanapith, Delhi.

Jayadhavala Office

The scripture *Kasāya Pāhuḍ* was published by Bharatvarsiya Digambara Jaina Sangha, Mathura in 16 volumes. Siddhāntācārya Paṇḍit Phulachandra Shastri made its commentary *Jayadhavalā Ṭikā* along with its editing and translation in Hindi at Jayadhavala office in Kāśī.

Tīrthaṅkara Mahāvīra Aur Unakī Ācārya Paramparā

This scripture was composed by Dr Nemicandra Shastri Ara. It was finalized at Sri Syadvad College, Bhadaini in the presence of Paṇḍit Kailash Chandra Shastri and Dr. Darabarilal Kothiya. Akhil Bharatiya Digambara Jaina Vidvat Parishad published it in four volumes.

Ramghat Jaina temple Library

There is an old library at Śvetāmbara Jaina temple situated at Ramghat in Kāśī. It has a collection of some handwritten scriptures. Probably the handwritten texts of Mahopādhyāya Yaśovijaya have also been found in this collection.

Library and Reading room of Bhelupur Digambara Jaina Temple

A library and reading room were established in the Digambara Jaina temple at Bhelupur, a few years ago.

Image of Goddess Padmāvatī

A splendid and artistic image of goddess Padmāvatī is erected in Khaḍgāsana Digambara Jaina temple at Bhelupur. Many people from outside are also devotees of this goddess.

Mahavira Press

Mahavira Press is established in Bhelupur area of Kāśī. It has published more than one thousand books belonging to Jaina *dharma*. Pandit Babulal Phagulla manages it. Vardhaman press and Sanmati Mudranalaya (Press) are also working as its branches. This press is about 40 years old.

Jaina branches in Universities of Kāśī

In the Department of Jaina-Bauddha Philosophy under the Sanskrit Vidya Dharma Vigyan faculty of Banaras Hindu University, Jaina philosophy is being taught at the post-graduate level. Several researchers have completed their research works here and attained the title of Chakravarti (Ph.D.). Similarly, under the Faculty of Art, in the Department of Philosophy, the students doing post-graduation in the subject of philosophy can attain their degree opting from the group of Jaina Philosophy in the final year, just as in the Faculty of Art in the Department of Sanskrit the students doing post-graduation in Sanskrit can attain their degree opting from the Jaina-Bauddha group in the final years. This group has not been running since a few years.

Under Sampurnanand Sanskrit University, in the faculty of Sramana Vidya, there are running two independent Departments — Jaina philosophies, and Prakrit and Jainagam. The degree in post-graduation can be achieved from these Departments and research work can also be done.

13

Sources of Jaina Time Measure

K.K. Jain

ACCORDING to Jainism the whole universe is created with six materials — the soul (*jīva*), *pudgala,* truth (*dharma*), non-truth (*adharma*), space and time (*kāla*). Universe is divided into two parts — cosmic space and non-cosmic space. In the non-cosmic space there exists sky and the rest of materials are absent, but in the cosmic sky all the aforesaid materials have been found.

All those which contain consciousness like the knowledge (wisdom) and observation, is soul. Besides, all the remaining materials are inanimate objects, generally called *pudgala*. In other philosophies both these objects are called lifeless (*jaḍa*) and conscious (*cetanā*) matters. According to Jainism, the inanimate or lifeless materials have been divided into five parts — *pudgala,* truth (*dharma*), non-truth (*adharma*), space and age (*kāla*). Thus, including soul there are six materials that have been accepted in the Jaina tradition, which comprise this nature and universe.

In this universe the visible world, which is separate from the soul endowed with wisdom and observation, is synonymous with *pudgala*. That which helps the soul and *pudgala* in its functioning is the truth (*dharma*) material. This material is totally different from the word *dharma* which is in vogue in the world. Similarly which hinders the soul and *pudgala,* is non-truth (*adharma*). It is also totally different from the word *adharma,* which is in vogue in the present world. In the modern scientific terminology these *dharma* and *adharma* materials can be assumed as the alternates of ether and space respectively. That which gives space to stay is the sky material. This is called Space in scientific terminology.

That which is the cause of every change happening at every moment in every material is the time material. Its works are — turning (*vartnā*), result (*pariṇāma*), action (*kriyā*), priority (*paratva*), posteriority (*aparatva*). Time is the shortest undivided unit of age (*kāla*) and its longest unit is *kalpakāla*. *Kalpakāla* cannot be measured and so it is also called countless years.

Again *kalpakāla* is divided into *utsarpiṇī* age and *avasarpiṇī* age. In the *utsarpiṇī* age, the pleasure and joy increases while in the *avasarpiṇī* age this is reduced. In fact, this difference between the two is due to the variations in the ascending and decending orders of pleasure and sorrow. If we do not think about the order then there is no difference between the two just like the dark half and bright half of every month, because moonlight remains the same in both the fortnights. Difference is only that in the bright half the brightness is in the ascending order and in the dark half its brightness is in descending order. Again, both the ages are divided into six spokes (*ārās*) each. In the *avasarpiṇī* age these are called 1. Suṣamā-Suṣamā, 2. Suṣamā, 3. Suṣamā-Duṣamā, 4. Duṣamā-Suṣamā, 5. Duṣamā, and finally 6. Duṣamā-Duṣamā. If we place these six in reverse order then these are the parts of the *utsarpiṇī* age 1. Duṣamā-Duṣamā, 2. Duṣamā, 3. Duṣamā-Suṣamā, 4. Suṣamā-Duṣamā, 5. Suṣama and 6. Suṣamā-Suṣamā. According to Jainism at present the fifth Duṣamā period of *avasarpiṇī* age is going on.

Among the twenty-four *tīrthaṅkaras* of Jaina *dharma*, in the modern age, Bhagavān Mahāvīra was the 24th *tīrthaṅkara*. He was born in the last phase of the fourth period. Bhagavān Mahāvīra dwelled at home for 30 years. After that he took initiation and performed a hard penance for 12 years. He attained the knowledge of salvation (*kevala jñāna*) and thereby delivering spiritual discourses he attained salvation (*mukti* or *nirvāṇa*) at Pāvāpur in modern Bihar at the age of 72. After 470 years of salvation (*nirvāṇa*) of Mahāvīra Svāmī the Vikram Saṁvat came into vogue :

> *vikkamarajjārambhā purao sirivīranivvuī bhaṇiyā* ।
> *sunna-muṇi-veya* (470) *jutto vikkama-kālāu jiṇakālo* ॥
> — *Sthavirāvalī* (*Merutuṅga*)

In the *Tiloyapaṇṇatti* (Vikram Saṁvat 540) composed by Yati Vṛṣabhācārya (fifth-sixth century), there have been found four opinions relating to the origin of the King Śaka after the attainment of salvation (*nirvāṇa*) by Mahāvīra. The original ballads (narratives) revealing these opinions are as under —

> *vīrajiṇe siddhigade cau-saya-igisaṭṭhi-vāsa parimāṇe* ।
> *kālammi adikkante uppaṇṇo ettha-saka-rāo* ॥
> *ahavā vīre siddhe, sahassa-ṇavakammi saga-sayabbhahie* ।
> *paṇasīdimmi yatīde paṇamāse saka-ṇio jādo* ॥
> *coddasa-sahassa-saga-saya-te ṇavadī-vāsa-kāla-vicchede* ।
> *vīresara-siddhīdo, uppaṇṇo saga-ṇio ahavā* ॥
> *ṇivvāṇe vīrajiṇe, chavvāsa-sadesu pañca-varisesuṁ* ।
> *paṇamāsesu gadesuṁ, saṁjādo saga-ṇio ahavā* ॥
> — *Tiloyapaṇṇatti* 4/1508-121

It means King Śaka was born after 461 years of *pramāṇa kāla*, after the attainment of salvation (*mukti*) by Vīra Jinendra. It can also be said that King Śaka was born 9785 years and five months after the attainment of salvation by Vīra Bhagavān; or he was born 14793 years after the attainment of salvation by Vīra Bhagavān or he was born 605 years and five months after the attaining of salvation by Vīra Bhagavān.

But among these opinions the last opinion that King Śaka was born 605 years and 5 months after the attaining of salvation (*nirvāṇa*) by Vīr Bhagavān is in consonance with the opinion expressed in *Sthavirāvalī* composed by Merūtuṅga. Thus, the aforesaid last opinion should be assumed correct for reckoning the period of Jaina because among the three possibilities mentioned by Ācārya Vīrsena,[1] the composer of commentary *Dhavalā Ṭīkā*, one of the opinions is that King Śaka was born 605 years and 5 months after the salvation (*nirvāṇa*) of Vīra Jinendra. This opinion has also been confirmed by the *Harivaṁśa Purāṇa*[2] composed by Jinasenācārya of the ninth century of Vikram Saṁvat. In the *Sāmaññaphala Sutta* of *Dīgha-Nikāya* composed in Pāli, the names of Makkhali Gośāla and Nigaṇṭha Nāṭaputta among the six *Tīrthaṅkaras* have been mentioned.[3] Even in the *Bhagavatī Sūtra*, Gośālaka and Mahāvīra are mentioned as rivals. Yet another reason for accepting this opinion is that this is in consonance with the Vīra *nirvāṇa* Saṁvat too, which is in vogue in the present Jaina society.

Generally, there are two prominent sources for reckoning the period of Jaina. As the first source, we can calculate the time on the basis of the tradition of the kings in those periods; as the second source we can calculate the time by taking into consideration the "*Sthaviras*" in the tradition of Bhagavān Mahāvīra that represent the period. Apart from it, Muni Kalyāṇa Vijaya has mentioned the third tradition treating the *Therāvalī*, composed by Ācārya Himavata, as its basis in which

---

1. *pañcayamāsā pāñca ya vāsā chacceva honti vāsasayā* ।
   sagakāleṇa ya sahiyā thāveyavvo tado rāsī ॥4 ॥
   gutti-payattha-bhayāmi coddasa rayaṇāi samaikantāī ।
   pariṇivvude jiṇinde to rājjaṁ sagaṇarindassa ॥42 ॥
   satta sahassā ṇavasada pañcāṇaudi sapañcamāsa ya ।
   aikaṅtā vāsāṇaṁ jaeyā taeyā saguppatī ॥43 ॥
   — *Ṣaṭkhaṇḍāgama*, pp. 132-33; *Jaina sāhitya ke itihāsa kī pūrvapīṭhikā*, p. 150, *Commentary*
2. *varṣāṇāṁ ṣaṭśatīṁ tyaktvā pañcāgrāṁ māsapañcakam* ।
   muktiṁ gate mahāvīre śakarājastato'bhavat ॥
   — *Harivaṁśa Purāṇa*, 60/551
3. *Dīgha Nikāya, Sāmaññaphalasutta*, 1/2.

the Jaina *ācāryas* in the tradition and their contemporary kings are included collectively.

Making the kings' tradition the basis of measuring the Jaina time from the Pradyota's time up to the Śaka's Kingdom and Vikram Saṁvat, Kailash Chandra Shastri is the first among all to have mentioned that the night on which Mahāvīra attained *nirvāṇa* on the same night Pālaka held throne of Magadha. After the Pālaka's rule of 60 years, the period of Nanda's rule has been described, which lasted for 155 years. According to the Purāṇas, from the period of Nandavardhana to the last Nanda ruler, the period extended for 123 years. Nandas ruled for these 123 years. Thus, the additional 32 years (155 - 123 = 32) lead us to a year or two ahead of the Udāyī's rule. It means that another period, beginning from the coronation of Udāyī is prominent just like the lineage of Pālaka, but in accordance to the Purāṇas, an interval of 64 years should be kept between the sixth year of Ajātaśatru's rule (coronation period of Pālaka) and the coronation of Udāyī.

According to the Jaina calculation, however, the ruling period of Pālaka is 60 years. Thus again there is a gap of four years in the period of Candragupta and his ascension to the throne about 215 or 219 years after the attaining of *nirvāṇa* by Mahāvīra. In this way varied dates are calculated. The ruling period of Mauryas has been divided into two groups of years — 108 years and 30 years. The first group of 108 years belong to the Maurya lineage and the second group of 30 years belong to Puṣyamitra. After this, 60 years of Bālamitra-Bhānumitra have been included. This calculation lead us to 413 years ahead of the attainment of *nirvāṇa* by Mahāvīra. After it, the period of 40 years has been said to be the ruling period of Nahapāna. The period of next 13 years belong to Gardabhilla's rule and the next 4 years to the Śaka's rule. All of these make 470 years in total (*Jaina Sāhitya Kā Itihāsa Pūrvapīṭhikā*, pp. 153-54).

The difference between Vikram Saṁvat and Anno Domini (AD) is 57 years and if we add this figure to the total of 470 years, then we get the number 527 which is in consonance with the opinion of the historians that Bhagavān Mahāvīra had attained *nirvāṇa* in 527 BC. Similarly, the difference of years between the Vikram Saṁvat and the Śaka Saṁvat is 135 years and if this figure is added to the number 470, then the total will be 605. This too confirms the aforesaid statement that Bhagavān Mahāvīra had attained *nirvāṇa* about 605 years before Śaka Saṁvat.

Against this calculation of time, making the mention of Ācārya Hemacandra their basis, some scholars like Dr. Harman Jakobi, Jarl Carpentier, Kashi Prasad, Jayasavala, Dr. Hernle have raised some objections. Paṇḍit Yugal-Kiśora Mukhtāra had removed those objections after a deep reflection. He has said that the present Vikram Saṁvat is the Saṁvat of the death of King Vikram, which began 470 years after the Vīra *nirvaṇa*. But most of the scholars do not agree with the opinion of Paṇḍit Yugal-Kiśora Mukhtāra, because the beginning of Vikram Saṁvat is generally assumed from the coronation of Vikram.

The 2500th *nirvāṇa* festival of Bhagavān Mahavīra was celebrated in 1973-74. So if we subtract 1973 from 2500 then the *nirvāṇa* year of Bhagavān Mahāvīra is accertained to 527 BC, which is aligned to the present belief.

Now let us analyse the second source of Jaina time calculation on the basis of the *sthaviras* representing the period. This source is assumed by the Śvetāmbara sect of Bhagavān Mahāvīra's tradition. From the salvation (*nirvāṇa*) time of Bhagavān Mahāvīra to the period of 605 years of Śaka Saṁvat, there had been 20 great personalities who attained the post of Saṅgha Sthavīra, whose humble life of householder, and their accomplishments representing the period have been mentioned in the *Sthavirāvalī* or *Yugapradhāna Paṭṭāvalī.*

Muni Kalyāṇa Vijaya has quoted narrations from the above-mentioned *Sthavirāvalī* which meant that after the attainment of salvation (*nirvāṇa*) by Mahāvīra, Sudharma for 20, Jambū for 44, Prabhava for 11, Svayambhava for 23, Yaśobhadra for 50, Sambhūti Vijaya for 8, Bhadrabāhu for 14 and Sthūlabhadra for 45 years, had held the post of *Yugapradhāna* respectively. Till here, a period 215 years have been past after Vīra's *nirvāṇa*.

After them Ārya Mahāgirī, Ārya Suhasti and Guṇa Sundara remained on the post of *Yugapradhāna* for 30, 46, and 44 years respectively. Thus, 335 years passed after Vīra *nirvāṇa*.

Thereafter, Nigoha Vyākhyātā Kālakācārya remained on the post of *Yugapradhāna* for 41 years and Śāṇḍilya for 38 years and thus 414 years passed after Vīra *nirvāṇa*.

Thereafter, Revatīmitra for 36 years and Ārya Maṅgu for 20 years remained on the post of *Yugapradhāna*. Till then 470 years passed after Vīra *nirvāṇa*. After them, Āryadharma for 27, Bhadragupta for 39, Śrīgupta for 15 and Vajra for 36 years remained on the post of *Yugapradhāna*. Thus, 584 years passed after Vīr *nirvāṇa*.

Thereafter, Āryarakṣita for 13 and Puṣyamitra for 20 years remained on the post of *Yugapradhāna*. Thus, a period of 605 years passed after the salvation (*nirvāṇa*) of Mahāvīra, and Śaka Saṁvat came into vogue.

Apart from the aforesaid two sources, Muni Kalyāṇavijaya has mentioned the third source also on the basis of *Therāvalī*, composed by Himavata. A long list of many kings and different influential Jaina *ācārya*s belonging to the periods after Vīra *nirvāṇa* has been mentioned. In between many historical incidents have also been mentioned which are significant from the viewpoint of history.

Only, a brief introduction of main sources of Jaina time calculation has been given here, which is a period of 605 years beginning from the period of salvation attained by Mahāvīra and extending up to the middle age of Śaka Saṁvat. For the remaining calculations of time the subsequent Vikram Saṁvat and Śaka Saṁvat are significant.

Bibliography

Harivaṁśa Purāṇa (Jinsenācārya), ed., Pannalal Jaina Sahityācārya, Kāśī: Bhāratīya Jñānapīṭha, Vikram Saṁvat 2019, Vīra Nirvāṇa Saṁvat-2488.

Jaina Sāhitya Kā Itihās (*History of Jaina litrature*), *Pūrvapīṭhikā*, Pandit Kailash Chandra Shastri, Varanasi: Sri Ganesh Varni Digambara Jaina Sansthana, Nariya, 2nd edn., 1996.

Prabandhakośa Kā Aitihāsika Vivecana, Dr. Pravesh Bharadvaj, Jaipur: Prakrit Bharati Academy, 1st edn., 1995.

Prācīna Bhāratīya Kāla Gaṇanā evam Pāramparika Saṁvatsara, Dr. Rama Ji Pandeya, 1st edn., 1080.

Tiloyapaññatti (*Yativṛṣabhācārya*), *Bhāṣā Ṭīkā-Āryikā 105 Śrī Viśuddhamatī Mātājī*, Alvar (Rajasthan): Śrī 1008 Candraprabh Digambara Jaina Atiśaya Kṣetra Deharā Tijārā — 301411 vol. 2, 2nd edn., Vikram Saṁvat 2054, Vīra Nirvāṇa Saṁvat 2523.

Vīr nirvāṇa Saṁvat Aur Jaina Kāla-Gaṇanā, Muni Kalyāṇa Vijaya, Jalaur (Mārvāḍ): K.V. Shastra Samiti, Saṁvat 1987, Vīra Nirvāṇa Saṁvat 2457.

Our Contributors

Dr. Bhanu Shankar Mehta
B - 37/67, Birdopur
Varanasi – 221 010

Sri Jamna Lal Jain
C/o Jain Book Centre
Jain Mandir
Sarnath, Varanasi

Dr. Kamalesh Jain
Deptt. of Jaina & Bauddha Darshan
Faculty of Sanskrit Learning & Theology
Banaras Hindu University
Varanasi – 221 005

Sri Kranti Kumar
19, Pratap Nagar
Mavaiya, Sarnath
Varanasi – 221 007

Prof. M.N.P. Tiwari
Head
Dept. of History of Art
Faculty of Arts
Banaras Hindu University
Varanasi – 221 005

Dr. Smt. Munni Pushpa Jain
Anekanta Bhavanam
B - 23/45-P-6, Sharda Nagar Colony
Opp. Santoshi Mata Mandir, Navabganj
Varanasi – 221 010

Dr. Phool Chand Jain
Anekanta Bhavanam
B - 23/45-P-6, Sharda Nagar Colony
Opp. Santoshi Mata Mandir, Navabganj
Varanasi – 221 010

Prof. R.C. Sharma
Hon. Director/Ācārya
Jñāna-Pravaha,
Centre for Cultural Studies & Research
South of Samne Ghat
Varanasi – 221 005

Dr. Sagar Mal Jain
C/o Sri Narendra Kumar Jain
Sagar Plywood Centre
Nai Sarak
Shajapur – 465 001 (M.P.)

Dr. S.M. Jain
B - 32/12
Naria
Varanasi – 221 005

Acharya Sharad Kumar Sadhak
B - 38/13-30, Navodit Nagar
Tulsipur
Varanasi – 221 010

Dr. Shanti Swaroop Sinha
Dept. of History of Art
Faculty of Arts
Banaras Hindu University
Varanasi – 221 005

Index

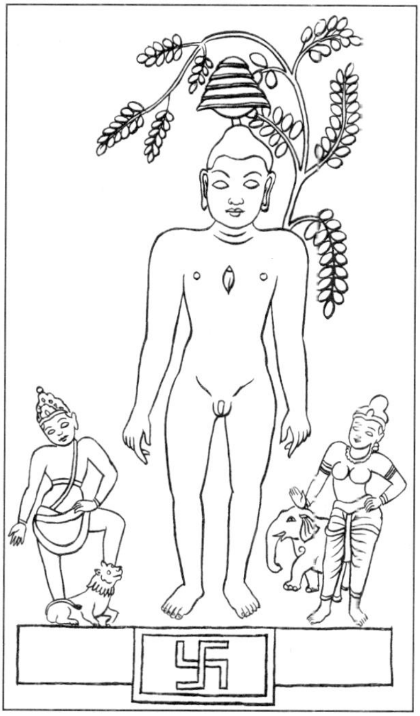

Fig. 4.1. Supārśvanātha.

Fig. 4.2. Candraprabhā.

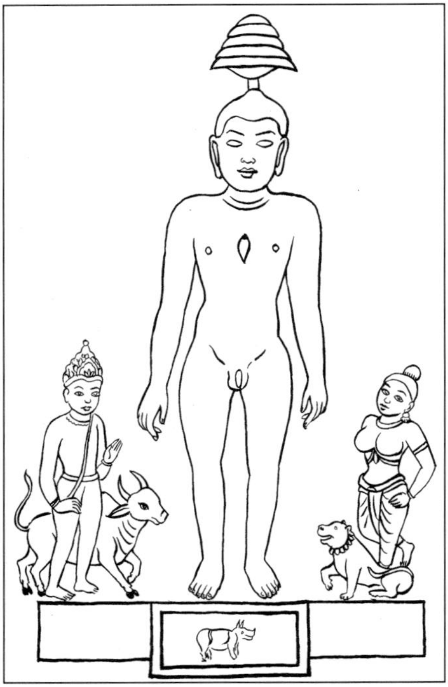

Fig. 4.3. Śreyāṁsanātha.

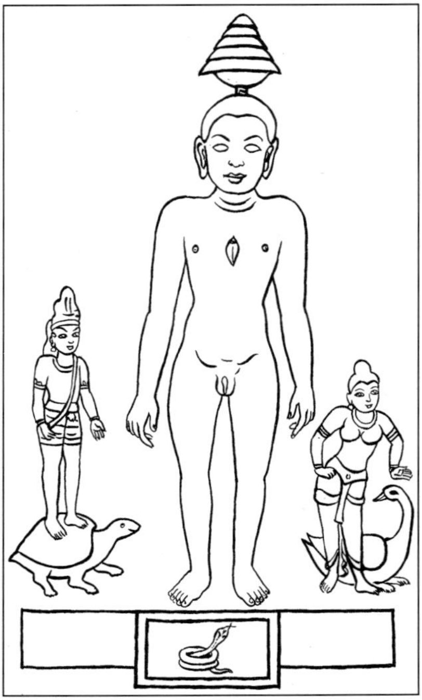

Fig. 4.4. Pārśvanātha.

Fig. 7.1. Tīrthaṅkara *c.* 7th century AD from Varanasi.

Fig. 7.2. Pārśvanātha *c*. 7th century AD from Varanasi.

Fig. 7.3. Pañcatīrthī *c*. 7th century AD from Varanasi.

Fig. 7.4. Padmaprabhā *c*. 10th century AD from Varanasi.

Fig. 7.5. Tīrthaṅkara *c.* 10th century AD from Varanasi.

Fig. 7.6. Tīrthaṅkara *c*. 10th century AD from Varanasi.

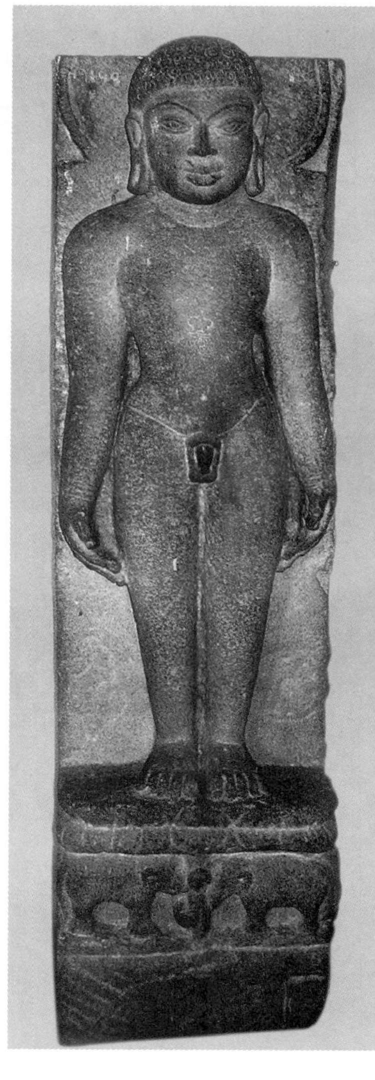

Fig. 7.7. Ajitanātha *c*. 7th century AD from Varanasi.